Latter-day Saint Women and the Priesthood of God

Also by the Author

*The Rise of the Mormons:
Latter-day Saint Growth in the 21st Century*
(LVX Publications, 2012;
second edition, forthcoming in Summer 2014)

*Of Masons and Mormons:
The Relationship Between
Freemasonry's Rituals of Initiation and the
Latter-day Saint Temple Ceremonies*
(LVX Publications, forthcoming in Spring 2014)

Latter-day Saint Women and the Priesthood of God

A Believer's Exploration

Mark Koltko-Rivera

Temple Spire Books
an imprint of
LVX Publications
New York City
2014

Copyright © 2014 Mark Koltko-Rivera. All rights reserved.

Except as permitted under the United States Copyright Act of 1976, no part of this publication may be reproduced or transmitted in any form or by any means, or stored in a database or retrieval system, without the prior written permission of the copyright holder.

Latter-day Saint Women and the Priesthood of God:
A Believer's Exploration
by Mark Koltko-Rivera
First edition, published April 2014 by Temple Spire Books,
an imprint of LVX Publications, New York City, 10019.

ISBN-13: 978-0-6159-9502-1   ISBN-10: 0-6159-9502-0
U.S. editions printed in the United States of America.

Front cover illustration: "Women move from darkness into light, receiving new knowledge and authority as Joseph Smith turns the key to them. [Detail of] illustration by Joseph A. F. Everett for the March 1936 cover of *Relief Society Magazine*" (as described by Derr, Cannon, & Beecher, 1992/2000, p. 47). The phrase in the illustration is taken from Joseph Smith's remarks as reported in the *Nauvoo Relief Society Minute Book* (1842-1844), page 40 (comma added).

Back cover author photo by Katherine Finkelstein: katherinefinkelstein.com

www.MarkKoltko-Rivera.com
authorMEKR@yahoo.com

Copies of this book may be purchased online at:
  http://astore.amazon.com/marswri-20

Booksellers: Check with your distributor for this book.

To B

truly an elect lady

Minutes of the Proceedings
of the
Third Meeting of the Society—

Lodge Room March 30th 1842.

Meeting opened with Singing—
Prayer by Prest. Joseph Smith—
The house full to overflowing.

Prest. J. Smith arose—spoke of the organization of the Society—said he was deeply interested that it might be built up to the Most High in an acceptable manner— ....

Said ...—that the Society should move according to the ancient Priesthood, hence there should be a select Society separate from all the evils of the world, choice, virtuous and holy—Said he was going to make of this Society a kingdom of priests as in Enoch's day—as in Pauls day— ....

—*Nauvoo Relief Society Minute Book*, page 22

[Joseph Smith] spoke of delivering the keys to this Society and to the church ...

[JS said] that the keys of the kingdom are about to be given to them [the sisters], that they may be able to detect every thing false—as well as to the Elders[.] ...

This Society is to get instruction thro' the order which God has established—thro' the medium of those appointed to lead—and I now turn the key to you in the name of God and this Society shall rejoice and knowledge and intelligence shall flow down from this time—this is the beginning of better days, to this Society[.]

—The Prophet Joseph Smith, April 28, 1842,
teaching at the sixth meeting of the Relief Society,
as recorded in *Nauvoo Relief Society Minute Book*, pages 37, 38, 40

Table of Contents

List of Figures	viii
Table	viii
Preface	ix
Introduction	3
1 What Joseph Smith Said About Women and the Priesthood	13
2 Justifications for Restricting LDS Priesthood to Men	41
3 Objections to Conferring Priesthood on LDS Women	61
4 The Real Reasons Why LDS Women Do Not Exercise the Priesthood in the Early 2010s	75
5 The Future	87
6 Further Objections	111
7 Summary and Conclusion	119
References	123
Illustration Credits	132
Index	133
About the Author	137

List of Figures

1-1	Joseph Smith turning the key to the Relief Society	23
1-2	Relationships between original documents, *Manuscript History*, and major publications of LDS history	33
2-1	The boundaries of the Roman Empire, about 60 AD.	54

Table

1-1	Frequency with which key phrases from Joseph Smith's 1842 remarks appear on the Church website.	30-31

Preface

In this book, I claim that there is no scriptural reason not to extend priesthood ordination to all worthy Latter-day Saint women. Statements by well-intended Church members to the effect that the Lord has restricted priesthood ordination to men are expressions of personal opinion, being neither supported by scripture nor explicit modern revelation. Arguments based on the idea that the Lord only ordained men are naïve regarding the way that the Lord seems to work with human cultures and social change. In modern times, it seems that Joseph Smith himself, during the last year and a half of his life, bestowed priesthood keys upon Latter-day Saint (LDS) women. Of course, I support all of this from the LDS Standard Works, modern revelations, and the valid historical record. I hope that this information will inform the private discussions that are going on around the Church at this time, regarding this issue.

I do not consider here the many impassioned arguments that people have made for and against the ordination of LDS women. I am interested in the views of One Personage only: The Lord, as expressed in His scriptures and through His prophets, when the latter are speaking as such. When I have looked very closely at these sources, I have found some interesting historical and doctrinal facts of which many of the Saints seem to be unaware today.

After a brief introductory chapter about the LDS priesthood, I consider teachings of the Prophet Joseph Smith that are only becoming widely known in this generation, on the subject of women and the priesthood (Chapter 1). I consider separately the justifications that have been advanced for restricting LDS ordination to men (Chapter 2), and the objections that have been advanced against conferring the LDS priesthood upon women (Chapter 3). I then explain the real reason why LDS women do not exercise the priesthood as of the early 2010s (Chapter 4). I describe what it is that might be best for the Saints to do—and *not* do—to address the issue of LDS women receiving the priesthood (Chapter 5). In Chapter 6, I consider more general objections—for example, objections to my even presuming to address this subject. Finally, I summarize my thoughts and relate some reflections on this issue (Chapter 7).

Some may think that part of what I say here can be applied to the matter of female ordination in other religious groups. However, let me state clearly and unequivocally that I have written this only in relation to the Latter-day Saints, without intending any application to other religious organizations.

Books of scripture are indicated in text and footnotes with the conventional abbreviations. As is the common practice today in quoting historical documents, I leave the original spelling, capitalization, and punctuation intact, without indicating "*(sic)*."

Why have I taken it upon myself to write about this controversial topic? First of all, because I am a faithful Latter-day Saint, and as such I take seriously what the Lord told the Saints through Joseph Smith the Prophet in Jackson County, Missouri, USA, on August 1st of 1831, when the Church itself was not quite 16 months old:

> For behold, it is not meet that I should command in all things; for he that is compelled in all things, the same is a slothful and not a wise servant; wherefore he receiveth no reward.
>
> Verily I say, men should be anxiously engaged in a good cause, and do many things of their own free will, and bring to pass much righteousness;
>
> For the power is in them, wherein they are agents unto themselves. And inasmuch as men do good they shall in nowise lose their reward.
>
> But he that doeth not anything until he is commanded, and receiveth a commandment with doubtful heart, and keepeth it with slothfulness, the same is damned. (Doctrine and Covenants 58:26-29)

I believe that striving for clarity in doctrine, and for honesty in how we describe doctrine, are very good causes.

Precisely because this topic is controversial, and because it is the subject of sometimes heated dispute amongst the Saints, it is important for the Saints to understand the true doctrinal and historical issues at stake here. Relatively few people seem to be publishing in print about this topic, as I do, from (1) a position of faith in the Gospel as taught by the Saints, (2) an awareness of scripture and its context, and (3) an understanding of some of the lesser-known truths of LDS history. It obligates those who *do* work from these combined positions to speak up and say something. I may be no one special, but I do have these characteristics.

I am a bit loathe to go into my qualifications, because Latter-day Saints tend to use this kind of information poorly. I have heard Saints give credence to a person's statements because the person is a faithful Saint, perhaps with an impressive history of offices in the Church, even though this person's grasp of scripture or its context is a bit shaky, and his or her logic is weak. I have also heard Saints discount the statements made by a person who has gone to the trouble of discovering important documentary evidence that has been ignored by many people who write about Church history—because this person's personal life may have been judged to be out of harmony with the Gospel.

It is unfortunate that so many of the Saints seem to judge the validity of a thought on the basis of the messenger, rather than the facts (including the scriptural foundations and context) and the logic behind that thought. This is particularly unseemly in a day when it is relatively easy to educate oneself regarding critical thinking and the detection of logical fallacy.[1]

But, as a people, we are where we are. So here, in brief, is the relevant background of the author of this book.

---

[1] See, for example, Gula (2002), and Paul & Elder (n.d.).

I am a convert to The Church of Jesus Christ of Latter-day Saints (hereafter simply "the Church"). Before my conversion, I had been a faithful member of another religious group, with which many members of my ancestral family had been affiliated for over one thousand years. One summer, just before my junior year of high school, having met some Latter-day Saints in the Northeast, and having received a copy of the Book of Mormon from them, I decided to put Moroni's promise[2] to the test; I studied, pondered, and went out into the woods of the southern tier of New York State to pray. Because I took Moroni's promise rather literally, and because at the time I was unfamiliar with the early 19th century idiom in which so much of the Book of Mormon is translated, I went out into the woods and prayed that the Lord would show me that the Book of Mormon "was not true"—because, despite how much I liked what it said, the book's doctrines conflicted with the teachings of the religious group to which I belonged. I was in for a surprise.

When I prayed out among the cedars of Rhinebeck, as I knelt and waited for an answer, I received into my heart a great feeling of peace that I had only rarely felt before, and there came into my mind a sensation that I can only describe as greater light. I received then and there a testimony of Joseph Smith as a prophet of God, of the Book of Mormon as God's word, and of The Church of Jesus Christ of Latter-day Saints as God's church; I received a reaffirmation of my already-existing conviction that God lives and that Jesus is the Christ, the Messiah, the divinely chosen Redeemer of the world. I came out of the woods with a very different religious orientation than that with which I had entered them. This was to be only the first of many subsequent spiritual experiences that have continued over the course of four decades to confirm the truth of the basic points of my testimony.

My family was not pleased. I was forbidden to study the Book of Mormon, to attend LDS services, or to meet with the LDS missionaries (all of which I did anyway, now and again, being the re-

---

2 Moroni 10:3-5.

bellious juvenile delinquent that I was). It was not until my sophomore year of college that my family permitted me to receive LDS baptism. After my senior year, during which I had submitted my mission papers, my mother stated her opposition to my serving a mission in very direct terms: "Mark, if you go on your mission, don't worry about your family. You don't have one." I went anyway, serving in the Japan Okayama Mission (1978-1980).

That was many years ago. My four children were all born under the covenant. I have served as a counselor in two bishoprics in Manhattan, and as a member of a stake high council in New Jersey. I have also served as a Sunday School teacher for the Gospel Doctrine class in perhaps five or six wards and branches over the years, in three of the U.S. states. I am an active and committed member of the Church today, and plan on being so the rest of my life.

I hold an undergraduate degree, majoring in psychology, from Haverford College, where I received an award for devising and executing a systematic study program in LDS history. I earned a master's degree from the Fordham University Graduate School of Education, and I hold an earned doctorate from the Department of Applied Psychology at New York University. I have published in scientific and humanities journals, am an elected Fellow of the American Psychological Association (APA), and have received several professional awards for my scholarly work, including the Margaret Gorman Early Career Award in the Psychology of Religion, from the Society for the Psychology of Religion and Spirituality (APA Division 36). For a living, I run a research firm, and am a writer.

What could the reader conclude from this? That I am a Latter-day Saint with a strong, spiritually based testimony. That I have more than a passing acquaintance with our scriptures, the teachings of our latter-day prophets, and LDS history. That I am not an intellectual lightweight. Together, that ought to be enough to at least lead the reader to consider my ideas seriously.

—Mark E. Koltko-Rivera
New York City
April 28, 2014
the 172nd anniversary of Joseph Smith's discourse
at the sixth meeting of the Nauvoo Female Relief Society

www.MarkKoltko-Rivera.com
E-mail: authorMEKR@yahoo.com

Acknowledgements

I am grateful to several individuals with whom I have discussed these ideas from time to time. I am also especially grateful to those who have encouraged me to endure, and helped to bear my burdens, through difficult times, some of which befell me during the course of writing this book. Of course, I bear sole responsibility for any errors of fact or interpretation in this book.

Latter-day Saint Women and the Priesthood of God

Introduction

This book is about Latter-day Saint women and the Priesthood of God. In order to set the stage for the discussion, here I share some thoughts about priesthood, what it is, and how it has come to the Church from ancient to modern times. I also explore the matter of priesthood keys, and how those have been passed along throughout Gospel history.

The Priesthood, Its Power, and Its Responsibilities

The Priesthood of God is a crucial aspect of the Gospel as taught by The Church of Jesus Christ of Latter-day Saints. As Joseph Smith put it, "the Priesthood is an everlasting principle."[3] Most adult LDS converts are taught the following concepts early in their association with the Church:

> The priesthood is the eternal power and authority of God. Through the priesthood, God created and governs the heavens and the earth. By this power the universe is kept in perfect order. Through this power He redeems and exalts His children, thereby accomplishing His work and glory, which is "to bring to pass the immortality and eternal life of man" (Moses 1:39).
>
> God gives His priesthood power to worthy male members of the Church so they can act in God's name for the salvation of the human family. Priest-

---

[3] J. F. Smith (1938) p. 157.

hood holders can be authorized to preach the gospel, administer the ordinances of salvation, and govern God's kingdom on earth.[4]

The priesthood is eternal in its timescale, all-encompassing in scope, and cosmic in scale. Its fundamental purpose is to further God's work for the salvation of the human family. In the service of that purpose, the priesthood can be used in many ways.

The priesthood as granted to human beings has great powers even over the physical universe, according to ancient scripture restored in modern times:

> For God having sworn unto Enoch and unto his seed with an oath by himself that every one being ordained after this order and calling should have power, by faith, to break mountains, to divide the seas, to dry up waters, to turn them out of their course;
>
> To put at defiance the armies of nations, to divide the earth, to break every band, to stand in the presence of God; to do all things according to his will, according to his command, subdue principalities and powers; and this by the will of the Son of God which was from before the foundations of the world.[5]

But such is not the major way in which the priesthood is used to further the salvation of humanity. In the detailed record of the Book of Mormon prophet Alma's discourse to the people of Ammonihah, Alma teaches powerfully of the qualifications required for ordination to the priesthood. However, when it comes to describing their responsibilities, he focuses on one thing only.

---

[4] Combined text from *Gospel Principles* (2009) p. 67 (Ch. 13, "The Priesthood") and *True to the Faith* (2004) p. 124 (entry, "Priesthood").

[5] Joseph Smith Translation [JST], Genesis 14:30-31. Found in the "Joseph Smith Translation" section of the Latter-day Saint edition of the Holy Bible, or online at https://www.lds.org/scriptures/jst .

> ... I would cite your minds forward to the time when the Lord God gave these commandments unto his children; and I would that ye should remember that the Lord God ordained priests, after his holy order, which was after the order of his Son, **to teach these things unto the people.**
>
> And those priests were ordained after the order of his Son in a manner that **thereby the people might know** in what manner to look forward to his Son for redemption. ...
>
> And thus being called by this holy calling, and ordained unto the high priesthood of the holy order of God, **to teach his commandments unto the children of men**, that they also might enter into his rest ...[6]

Certainly, in the Lord's description to Joseph Smith of the responsibilities of various priesthood offices, the matter of teaching the Gospel and encouraging people to personal righteousness predominates.[7] We also learn from latter-day scriptures that the power of the Melchizedek Priesthood can be exercised specifically through ordinances, for the sake of our salvation and exaltation. As the Lord revealed to Joseph Smith in 1832:

> And this greater priesthood administereth the gospel and holdeth the key of the mysteries of the kingdom, even the key of the knowledge of God.
>
> Therefore, in the ordinances thereof the power of godliness is manifest.
>
> And without the ordinances thereof, and the authority of the priesthood, the power of godliness is not manifest unto men in the flesh;

---

[6] Alma 13:1-2, 6.
[7] D&C 20:38-59.

> For without this no man can see the face of God,
> even the Father, and live.[8]

There is much else that we learn about the priesthood in the scriptures, particularly in the Doctrine and Covenants. There are ethical guidelines for the exercise of the priesthood that are ignored at one's peril.[9] There is an array of priesthood offices, each with an intricate set of responsibilities.[10] There are priesthood temple ordinances that are essential to exaltation from the human mortal state to a godlike state, after death.[11] By the power and authority of the priesthood, evil spirits may be cast out.[12] But from what I have given so far in detail in just these few pages, it is clear that the priesthood is foundational, both to the functioning of the Church, and to the fulfillment of the purposes of God.

Priesthood Keys

Power without direction is chaos. The priesthood without direction would not fulfill its purpose of furthering the salvation of the human family; indeed, it might well impede the fulfillment of that purpose. So it is that we have keys to the priesthood, the power to direct the priesthood for certain specific purposes. No priesthood act is valid unless it is done in accordance with the direction provided by those who hold the keys.

The keys of the priesthood are many, and differ in scope. The keys held by the bishop of a ward are quite different in scope from those held by the President of the Church.

The all-encompassing concept, 'the keys of the kingdom,' comprises all the priesthood keys that are available to mortal priesthood holders at any given time. The term "keys of the kingdom" occurs

---

[8] D&C 84:19-22.
[9] D&C 121:34-46.
[10] For example, see D&C Sections 20, 84, and 107.
[11] D&C 124:25-41; 132: 19-24.
[12] D&C 50:26-33.

exactly once in the Bible. The Lord has asked Peter who Peter thinks Jesus is. Peter responds that Jesus is the true Messiah. Jesus points out that Peter received this knowledge through revelation from the Father, and that it is upon this rock of revelation that Jesus shall build His Church. The Lord then tells Peter:

> And I will give unto thee the keys of the kingdom of heaven: and whatsoever thou shalt bind on earth shall be bound in heaven: and whatsoever thou shalt loose on earth shall be loosed in heaven.[13]
>
> ...
>
> And after six days Jesus taketh Peter, James, and John his brother, and bringeth them up into an high mountain apart,
>
> And was transfigured before them: and his face did shine as the sun, and his raiment was white as the light.
>
> And behold, there appeared unto them Moses and Elias[14] talking with them.[15]

The Prophet Joseph Smith taught that this was an occasion for the bestowal of priesthood keys:

> The Priesthood is everlasting. The Savior, Moses, and Elias gave the keys to Peter, James, and John, on the mount, when they were transfigured before him.[16]

There are also keys that are very specific in nature. In modern times, Joseph Smith reported that he had received priesthood keys when he and Oliver Cowdery, praying in the Kirtland Temple on April 3, 1836, were visited in vision by the Lord, Moses, Elias, and Elijah. In relation to the latter three visitors, Joseph reported:

---

[13] Matthew 16:19.
[14] Here, "Elias" is used as the Greek form of the name "Elijah."
[15] Matthew 17:1-3.
[16] *History of the Church* (1902-1932) vol. 3, p. 387. Also quoted in J. F. Smith (1938) p. 158.

> ... the heavens were again opened unto us; and Moses appeared before us, and committed unto us the keys of the gathering of Israel from the four parts of the earth, and the leading of the ten tribes from the land of the north.
>
> After this, Elias appeared, and committed the dispensation of the gospel of Abraham, saying that in us and in our seed all generations after us should be blessed.
>
> And after this vision had closed, another great and glorious vision burst upon us; for Elijah the prophet, who was taken to heaven without tasting death, stood before us, and said:
>
> Behold, the time has fully come, which was spoken of by the mouth of Malachi—testifying that he [Elijah] should be sent, before the great and dreadful day of the Lord come—
>
> To turn the hearts of the fathers to the children, and the children to the fathers, lest the whole earth be smitten with a curse—
>
> Therefore, the keys of this dispensation are committed into your hands; and by this ye may know that the great and dreadful day of the Lord is near, even at the doors.[17]

Several members of the Quorum of the Twelve left testimonies that, at a meeting in March of 1844, Joseph Smith committed the keys to the Twelve, just two months before his assassination. As Brigham Young taught five months after this meeting:

> Joseph conferred upon our heads all the keys and powers belonging to the Apostleship which he himself held before he was taken away, and no man or

---

[17] D&C 110:11-16. Square brackets in original.

set of men can get between Joseph and the Twelve in this world or in the world to come.[18]

One year after the March 1844 meeting, Elder Parley P. Pratt of the Twelve published this in the *Millennial Star*:

> Said he [Joseph Smith], 'I know not why; but for some reason I am constrained to hasten my preparations, and to confer upon the Twelve all the ordinances, keys, covenants, endowments, and sealing ordinances of the priesthood, and so set before them a pattern in all things pertaining to the sanctuary [the temple] and the endowment therein.'[19]

Perhaps the most detailed account of the March 1844 meeting is the one of Wilford Woodruff, who was a member of the Twelve at the time. Writing as the President of the Church in 1892, he stated:

> I remember the last speech that [Joseph Smith] ever gave us before his death. . . . He stood upon his feet some three hours. ... He laid before us our duty .... and in his remarks to us he said: 'I have had sealed upon my head every key, every power, every principle of life and salvation that God has ever given to any man who ever lived upon the face of the earth. And these principles and this Priesthood and power belong to this great and last dispensation which the God of Heaven has set His hand to establishing the earth. Now, said he, addressing the Twelve, 'I have sealed upon your heads every key, every power, and every principle which the Lord has sealed upon my head.'[20]

---

[18] *Teachings of Presidents ... Joseph Smith* (2007) p. 534.
[19] *Teachings of Presidents ... Joseph Smith* (2007) p. 534.
[20] *Teachings of Presidents ... Joseph Smith* (2007) p. 532. Brackets in original.

Where This All Leaves Us

I believe all of this. It is part of my testimony. The idea that God would delegate some of His authority to humans to accomplish His purposes makes perfect sense to me; as my children grew, they were given greater authority, partly to *help* them grow, and so it stands to reason that God would do something similar. As far as the miraculous powers ascribed to the priesthood are concerned—well, I have witnessed personally some of these powers at work.

I believe that all of this has been instituted by God for our benefit. However, there is an aspect of the way that the priesthood has been implemented in our day that has raised questions for me. It has to do with the practice of the Church wherein the priesthood is not conferred upon women.

Like many other members of the Church, I have heard many times that the Lord set things this way. What I have not heard is a shred of support for these statements, from either the scriptures or the words of the prophets when they undeniably are speaking as such. Like many members of the Church, I have heard these claims, and I have asked, "Where does it say that?" All of this leads me to ask, more formally:

> Where does it say, in the Standard Works or modern revelation, that the priesthood is not to be conferred upon women, or that women are not to be ordained to priesthood offices?

I set out some time ago to seek for answers to this question. I set forth in this book what I have found, what I have pondered, and what I have concluded.

There is one issue that I do *not* address in this book. This is the idea that many LDS women *already* have the priesthood, by virtue of their having received the temple endowment.[21]

---

[21] This is a position held by Quinn (1992) and some other scholars.

I have chosen not to engage this issue, in order to focus more clearly on what are, to me, logically prior issues: Has the Lord restricted the priesthood to men? Conversely, has the Lord barred women from the priesthood? If neither of these things is true, then why do so many Latter-day Saints believe and teach that the priesthood is not to be conferred upon women?

It should be clear from what I have said earlier in this Introduction that priesthood is a central concept in the LDS faith. In such a context, the question of who actually may hold that priesthood is an important one.

1

What Joseph Smith Said About Women and the Priesthood

Appropriately enough, this is a chapter of firsts. When it comes to matters of LDS doctrine and practice, Joseph Smith should get the first word, as he does so here. In addition, for many readers, this will be the first time that they have read most of the teachings of the Prophet Joseph that I present here—teachings that are monumental in their implications.

A word of advice, if you please. When you read what Joseph Smith said, do not give in to the impulse to try to make his words fit with the practices of the Church as we know them today.[22] Rather, read these words to discover what Joseph taught. For most Church members, these statements of the Prophet are tantamount to "lost teachings" of Joseph Smith. Try reading them for their plain sense meaning. You will discover interesting things.

Teachings of Joseph Smith, March and April 1842

Joseph Smith organized the Relief Society on March 17, 1842.[23] At the third meeting of the Relief Society, on March 31, 1842,[24] Jo-

---

[22] Technically, that process is known as "retroactive continuity," an instance of which is known as a "retcon." Retcons makes for more interesting comic book stories, and allowed Sherlock Holmes to return alive from the Reichenbach Falls, but they make for an exceptionally poor understanding of history.

[23] *Nauvoo Relief Society Minute Book* (1842-1844) pp. 6-15.

seph Smith spoke to the sisters of the Society, in a meeting that was reportedly "full to overflowing."[25] According to the minutes of the meeting, the Prophet said:

> ... that **the Society should move according to the ancient Priesthood**, hence there should be a select Society separate from all the evils of the world, choice, virtuous and holy—**Said he was going to make of this Society a kingdom of priests as in Enoch's day—as in Pauls day** ....[26]

At the sixth meeting of the Relief Society, held on April 28, 1842, the Prophet Joseph was in attendance again. As the minutes of the meeting put it:

> President Smith arose and said that the purport of his being present on the occasion was, to **make observations respecting the Priesthood, and give instructions for the benefit of the Society** ....[27]
>
> ...
>
> He continued to read the Chap. [1 Corinthians chapter 12] and give instructions respecting the different offices, and the necessity of every al acting in the sphere allotted him or her; and filling the several offices to which they were appointed—

---

[24] Mistakenly recorded in the minutes of the meeting as occurring on March 30th (Hedges et al., 2011, p. 48 note 173).
[25] *Nauvoo Relief Society Minute Book* (1842-1844) p. 22.
[26] *Nauvoo Relief Society Minute Book* (1842-1844) p. 22, emphases added. Joseph's statement is also reported in Ehat & Cook (1980/1991) p. 110.
[27] *Nauvoo Relief Society Minute Book* (1842-1844) p. 34, emphasis added. Joseph Smith's remarks, here and below, are also reported in Ehat & Cook (1980/1991) pp. 114-119.

Spoke of the disposition of man, to consider the lower offices in the church dishonorable and to look with jealous eyes upon the standing of others—that it was the nonsense of the human heart, for a person to be aspiring to other stations than appointed of God—that it was better for individuals to magnify their respective callings, and wait patiently till God shall say to them come up higher.

He said the reason of these remarks being made, was, that some little thing was circulating in the Society, that some persons were not going right in laying hands on the sick &c. Said if he had common sympathies, would rejoice that the sick could be heal'd, that the time had not been before, that these things could be in their proper order—that **the church is not now organiz'd in its proper order, and cannot be until the Temple is completed**—Prest. Smith continued the subject by adverting to the commission given to the ancient apostles "Go ye into all the world" &c.—no matter who believeth; these signs, such as healing the sick, casting out devils &c. should follow all that believe whether male or female. **He ask'd the Society if they could not see by this sweeping stroke, that wherein they are ordained, it is the privilege of those set apart to administer in that authority which is confer'd on them—and if the sisters should have faith to heal the sick, let all hold their tongues, and let every thing roll on.**

He said, if God has appointed him, and chosen him as an instrument to lead the church, why not let him lead it through? Why stand in the way, when he is appointed to do a thing? **Who knows the mind of God? Does he not reveal things differently from what we expect?** He remark'd that he was continually rising—altho' he had every thing bearing him down,—standing in his way and opposing—after all he always comes out right in the end.

Respecting the female laying on hands, he further remark'd, there could be no devils in it if God gave his sanction by healing—that there could be no more sin in any female laying hands on the sick than in wetting the face with water—that it is no sin for any body to do it that has faith, or if the sick has faith to be heal'd by the administration.

He reprov'd those that were dispos'd to find fault with the management of concerns—saying if he undertook to lead the church he would lead it right—that he calculates to organize the church in proper order &c. ....[28]

He said as he had this opportunity, he was going to instruct the Society and point out the way for them to conduct, that they might act according to the will of God—that he did not know as he should have many opportunities of teaching them—that they were going to be left to themselves,—they would not long have him to instruct them—that the church would not have his instruction long, and the world would not be troubled with him a great while, and would not have his teachings—**He spoke of delivering the keys to this Society and to the church**—that according to his prayers God had appointed him elsewhere[.]

He exhorted the sisters always to concentrate their faith and prayers for, and place confidence in those whom God has appointed to honor, whom God has plac'd at the head to lead—that we should arm them with our prayers.—**that the keys of the**

---

[28] *Nauvoo Relief Society Minute Book* (1842-1844) pp. 35-36, emphases added, paragraph breaks added.

1: What Joseph Smith Said About Women & Priesthood 17

> kingdom are about to be given to them, that they[29] may be able to detect every thing false—as well as to the Elders[.] ...[30]
>
> This Society is to get instruction thro' the order which God has established—thro' the medium of those appointed to lead—and **I now turn the key to you in the name of God and this Society shall rejoice and knowledge and intelligence shall flow down from this time**—this is the beginning of better days, to this Society[.] ...[31]
>
> **Prest. S. then offered instruction respecting the propriety of females administering to the sick by the laying on of hands said it was according to revelation** &c. said he never was plac'd in similar circumstances, and never had given the same instruction.[32]

Lest there be any thought that the minutes of the meeting are somehow a distortion of the Prophet Joseph's remarks, here is how the meeting is reported in the Prophet's journal entry for 28 April 1842:

> Thursday 28 at Two o'clock after-noon met the members of the "Female relief Society" and after presiding at the admission of many new members. **Gave a lecture on the pries[t]hood shewing how the Sisters would come in possession of the priviliges & blesings & gifts of the priesthood**—& that the signs should follow them. such as healing the sick casting out devils &c. & that they might attain unto. these

---

[29] That is, the Sisters.
[30] *Nauvoo Relief Society Minute Book* (1842-1844) pp. 37-38, emphases added.
[31] *Nauvoo Relief Society Minute Book* (1842-1844) p. 40, emphasis added.
[32] *Nauvoo Relief Society Minute Book* (1842-1844) p. 41, emphasis added.

blessings. by a virtuous life & conversation & diligence in keeping all the commandments[.]³³

What Did Joseph Smith Mean?

What did Joseph Smith mean when he said these things? And what implications do they have for the Church today? Below, I consider four of these statements, what they mean, and what impact they might have for the Latter-day Saints today.

Statement #1: "Said he was going to make of this Society a kingdom of priests as in Enoch's day—as in Pauls day"

Joseph Smith said this at the third meeting of the Relief Society, held on March 31, 1842, with the minutes being recorded by Eliza R. Snow (who would become Joseph's plural wife within about three months). The plain sense of this statement is that Joseph Smith intended to make of the Relief Society "a kingdom of priests."³⁴ Joseph also implied that such kingdoms of priests existed in the time of the ancient prophet Enoch, and in the days of Paul the apostle.³⁵

Did Joseph use this phrase the way it is used in the scriptures? The phrase, "a kingdom of priests," occurs in the Exodus narrative, before the giving of the Ten Commandments. The Israelites were just three months past their liberation from Egypt, and were camped before the mount in Sinai.

> And Moses went up unto God, and the LORD called unto him out of the mountain, saying, Thus shalt

---

[33] Hedges, Smith, & Anderson (2011) p. 52, emphasis added. See also: Ehat & Cook (1980/1991) p. 119; *History of the Church* (1908) v. 4 p. 602.

[34] "Priest" as a term technically covers either males or females, much like the words "actor" or "poet," even though purely feminine equivalents exist: "priestess," "actress," "poetess".

[35] A close analysis of Joseph Smith's statement about "a kingdom of priests" by Julie M. Smith (2014) is available online.

1: What Joseph Smith Said About Women & Priesthood

thou say to the house of Jacob, and tell the children of Israel;

Ye have seen what I did unto the Egyptians, and how I bare you on eagles' wings, and brought you unto myself.

Now therefore, if ye will obey my voice indeed, and keep my covenant, then ye shall be a peculiar treasure unto me above all people: for all the earth is mine.

And you shall be unto me **a kingdom of priests**, and an holy nation. These are the words which thou shalt speak unto the children of Israel.[36]

The Hebrew text here is מַמְלֶכֶת כֹּהֲנִים *mamlechet kohanim*, and it is well and literally rendered by the King James translators as "a kingdom of priests," a rendering also used by the Jewish Publication Society translators in our day.[37] In ancient times, when Jewish scholars translated their Bible into Greek (creating the Septuagint), they rendered this passage as βασίλειον ἱεράτευμα *basileion hierateuma* (again, a solid and literal translation).[38] It is this phrase from the Septuagint that Peter quotes when he states

But ye are a chosen generation, **a royal priesthood**, an holy nation, a peculiar people; that ye should shew forth the praises of him who hath called you out of darkness into his marvellous light:[39]

The phrase used here, "a royal priesthood," might have been rendered "a kingdom of priests," if only those King James translators on the right hand (working on Peter's letters) had known what those King James translators on the left hand (working on Exodus) were doing.

---

[36] Exodus 19:3-6; emphasis added.
[37] *JPS Hebrew-English Tanakh* (1999) Exodus 19:6.
[38] *Septuaginta* [LXX] (1979) Exodus 19:6.
[39] 1 Peter 2:9; emphasis added.

So here we have a phrase, "a kingdom of priests," that is used in Moses's day before the golden calf incident (and hence does not reflect the Mosaic Law), as well as in the days of the original apostles in the Meridian of time. The phrase is literally translated from the underlying scriptural languages in both the Old Testament and the New of the King James Version. My point: there is no way to wriggle around the literal meaning of the scriptural phrase by alleging some kind of mistake on the part of the King James translators.

> **The plain implication here is that Joseph Smith really *did* plan to make the Relief Society sisters into a kingdom of priests, a dominion in which most everyone held the priesthood.**

This compelling statement of Joseph Smith's was understood in its literal sense for many years among officials in the Relief Society. In June 1905, the fourth president of the general Relief Society, Sister Bathsheba W. Smith, made remarks that reflected this understanding at the first annual conference of the Pioneer Stake Relief Society. As she put it:

> I have always been pleased that I had my endowments when the Prophet lived.... I never like to hear a sermon without hearing something of the Prophet, for he gave us everything, every order of the priesthood .... He said he had given the sisters instructions that they could administer to the sick and he wanted to make us, as the women were in Paul's day, **"A kingdom of priestesses."**[40]

Sister Smith knew very well the precise wording of Joseph Smith's words as given in the *Nauvoo Relief Society Minute Book*; indeed, at this point, she had the *Minute Book* in her possession. All that she was doing was give the word "priests" its feminine form, thereby making more explicit the meaning Joseph clearly meant.

---

[40] "R.S. Reports: Pioneer Stake," (1905) p. 14; emphasis added.

Where does Enoch come into this story? We still know little about Enoch; most of what we know is contained in the Pearl of Great Price, in the Book of Moses, chapters 6 and 7, revealed to Joseph Smith in November and December of 1830. At least a year later, the Lord revealed to Joseph Smith, "These things were all written in the book of Enoch, and are to be testified of in due time."[41] The Lord has not yet revealed the pristine Book of Enoch to the world or the Church. When He does, we shall learn more about the "kingdom of priests" that Joseph implied existed in Enoch's day.

And Paul? What we know about the early Church, beyond the book of Acts, is derived from a small, perhaps random, sample of letters written by some early Church leaders, primarily Paul. Again, when we have the full record of the early Church, we shall learn more about "the kingdom of priests" that existed in Paul's day.

As I read Joseph Smith's statement, he was *not* implying that there were kingdoms of female priesthood holders in Enoch's or Paul's days. Rather, it was Joseph's intent to make the Relief Society a kingdom of priests, having the same power and authority that the kingdoms of priests in Enoch's and Paul's days had. That is quite a stunning statement for the Prophet Joseph to have made.

Statements #2 and #3: "He spoke of delivering the keys to this Society and to the church …. that the keys of the kingdom are about to be given to them, that they may be able to detect everything false — as well as to the Elders[.]"

Joseph Smith said this at the sixth meeting of the Relief Society, held on April 28, 1842. The full context of this statement, given above, makes clear that Joseph was saying that the keys of the kingdom were about to be given to the presidency of the Relief Society. I say this because it has been established that keys are not bestowed upon organizations, but upon individuals leading organizations.[42] Thus, when Joseph "spoke of delivering keys … to the church," he

---

41 D&C 107:57.
42 Oaks (1992).

was talking about bestowing the keys upon the leadership of the Church, the Quorum of the Twelve (upon whom Joseph bestowed the keys to the kingdom two years later, in March 1844; see the Introduction). Similarly, when Joseph "spoke of delivering keys to this [Relief] Society," he was talking about bestowing the keys upon the leadership of the Relief Society, including its president, Emma Smith. These statements are nothing short of stunning in their implications.

What did Joseph Smith mean by this? Allow me to point out a few of the more likely possibilities.

For Joseph to say that he was about to deliver the keys of the kingdom to the leadership of the Relief Society is *not* to say that he was about to deliver *all* the keys to them. He might have meant to say that he was about to deliver certain keys to the leadership of the Relief Society, and certain keys to the leadership of the Church as a whole. He might even have meant that (some?) keys were to be held *jointly* by the leadership of the Relief Society and the leadership of the male priesthood holders. ("But you can't have more than one group of people holding the keys!" I hear people say. Really? Where does it say that?)

No matter how we slice this pie, the plain sense meaning of Joseph's statements is that he was about to bestow the keys of the kingdom (some or all) upon the presidency of the Relief Society. And this, too, is monumental for Joseph to have said.

Statement #4: "I now turn the key to you in the name of God"

The Prophet said that "I now turn the key to you in the name of God," where "you" clearly indicated the leadership of the Relief Society.[43] An artist's conception of this is depicted in Figure 1-1.

---

[43] I am not the first to make this interpretation. The historian Linda King Newell (1985, p. 22, emphasis in original) has noted in relation to this passage in the *Nauvoo Relief Society Minute Book*:
> It is important to remember that "keys" were commonly associated with "priesthood" and that Joseph turned the key *to*

> The plain sense of this and the previous two statements is that Joseph Smith actually *did* convey one or more of the keys of the kingdom to the presidency of the Relief Society in April 1842.

Figure 1-1. Joseph Smith turning the key to the leaders of the Relief Society. (Source: Detail of *Relief Society Magazine*, March 1936, front cover, by Joseph A. F. Everett. Public domain.)

The existence of this illustration proves one thing conclusively, and suggests another quite powerfully. First, it conclusively proves that knowledge of the words actually said by Joseph Smith, as recorded in the *Nauvoo Relief Society Minute Book*, persisted among at least some members of the Church into the mid-1930s, over a generation after the *Minute Book* passed into the Church Archives at the death of Relief Society President Bathsheba W. Smith in 1910. Second, it strongly suggests that those who commissioned the illustration understood Joseph's words to mean "turn the key *over to*" and not "turn the key on behalf of."

---

women rather than in their behalf as the standard *History of the Church* would report (HC 4:607).

But Do Joseph Smith's Words Really Mean That?

I can well imagine that some readers might question whether the plain sense of Joseph Smith's words reflects his real meaning. Very well. Let us take a look at how some others have interpreted these words.

One LDS author has stated the following regarding Joseph's remarks on April 28, 1842:

> [Joseph Smith] delivered a message that has at times been misinterpreted or misunderstood because he used the word *keys* in *two* ways: first, by referring to priesthood keys, which he exercised in behalf of the sisters; and second, by referring to the keys of knowledge and power that provide those who are endowed in the temple with direct access to God.[44]
>
> ...
>
> The second way in which the Prophet used the word keys in his April 28 sermon to the Relief Society referred to keys of knowledge and power obtained by those endowed in the temple. In this usage, the Prophet was not referring to priesthood keys held by priesthood leaders, and he was not suggesting that Relief Society leaders would receive priesthood keys.[45]

The question that arises when I read such interpretations is, how does that author know the proper interpretation of Joseph Smith's remarks, beyond their face meaning? How does that author know that Joseph was using the same word, "keys," in two ways—and not just one? Frankly, the interpretation above sounds too much to me as if we were trying to fit what Joseph Smith said in the past into what we think he *should* have said, based on the practice of the

---

[44] Dew (2013) Kindle locations 2339-2341, emphases in original.
[45] Dew (2013) Kindle locations 2352-2355, footnote omitted.

Church in the present. This is an example of the process that I called "retroactive continuity" earlier (p. 13, footnote). What we have in the above author's interpretation thus seems to me to be a *retcon*—and, as I said earlier, retcons make for exceptionally poor understanding of what actually happened in history.

I have reproduced the Prophet Joseph's remarks above in some detail and in context for all to see. The secretary taking the minutes, Eliza R. Snow, said that the Prophet "spoke of delivering the keys to this Society and to the church." The secretary quoted Joseph as saying that "the keys of the kingdom are about to be given to them," in a context that clearly means to the leadership of the Sisters as distinguished from that of the Elders.

An especially interesting part of Joseph's remarks states that "I now turn the key to you in the name of God …." Of course, the plain sense meaning of the phrase "turn the key to you" is identical to that of the phrase "turn the key *over* to you."

It seems that a lot of energy has been expended to turn attention away from the plain sense meaning of this inconvenient phrase. For example, the LDS author quoted above noted the following in relation to Joseph's "turn the key to you" statement:

> About this meeting, Elder George A. Smith recorded: "[Joseph] spoke of delivering the keys of the Priesthood to the Church, and said that the faithful members of the Relief Society should receive them in connection with their husbands, that the Saints whose integrity has been tried and proved faithful, might know how to ask the Lord and receive an answer" (History of the Church, 4:604).[46]

The problem with this account of the Prophet's remarks is that everything about it is either misleading or outright inaccurate—no doubt, in a completely unintentional way. Let me explain.

---

[46] Dew (2013) Kindle location 2748 n. 47.

It is true that the *History of the Church*, vol. 4, pg. 604, does report the Prophet Joseph's remarks in the way noted above. It is also true that Elder George A. Smith composed this report, as it was he who was given the responsibility of compiling much of the *Manuscript History* of the Church—ten years after Joseph Smith's death—and it was the *Manuscript History* that formed the basis of the *History of the Church* about half a century later.

However, Elder George A. Smith did not "record" Joseph's remarks in the sense of an eyewitness. In fact, Elder George A. Smith is not listed among those who attended the April 28th, 1842 Relief Society meeting.[47] What Elder George A. Smith "recorded" was only *his own sense* of what Joseph Smith said, apparently using as his only source the very *Nauvoo Relief Society Minute Book* from which I have liberally quoted above. It is not that the *Nauvoo R.S. Minute Book* is some sort of defective record; rather, Elder George A. Smith used that record to devise his own version of events—a version that simply is not accurate, given what is actually in the *Minute Book*. Elder Geo. A. Smith's version reflects what the practice of the Church was in Elder Geo. A. Smith's own time. In short, what Elder George A. Smith wrote was a retcon.

In short, there is nothing in the annals of the Church that contradicts the plain sense meaning of what Joseph Smith taught to the Nauvoo Relief Society in the Spring of 1842. Statements that have been made to the contrary seem to be based on faulty historical understandings, supported by "retconned" published histories that have distorted Joseph's remarks for a century and a half.

Implications of Joseph Smith's 1842 Teachings to the Nauvoo Relief Society

There is a plain sense meaning to Joseph Smith's words that is clear for all to see. Those who wish to advance a different interpretation are welcome to do so—but they need to face the fact that they

---

[47] *Nauvoo Relief Society Minute Book* (1842-1844) p. 34.

bear a fairly heavy burden of proof if they wish to go against the rather obvious, plain-sense meaning of Joseph's words. And the plain-sense meaning of Joseph's words is that he intended to make of the Relief Society a kingdom of priests, and that he did turn one or more keys of the kingdom to the Relief Society presidency.

Joseph Smith did not leave us with a neat, cut-and-dried set of guidelines here. As I describe below, Joseph would revisit areas of doctrine and practice again and again over time, as his own understanding increased 'line upon line, precept upon precept,' and so his teaching of doctrine or application of practice became deeper, more mature, more articulated, more complex. But Joseph died before he could do that with the teachings he left the Relief Society in 1844 (a point to which I return later). Instead, Joseph left to the Church in these teachings a few broad strokes of doctrine—doctrine that has locked up in an archive for over a century, and which has now reemerged in just such an era in which it could be widely implemented. In a sense, Joseph left us with a test, a test that has been waiting for generations to us to take. It remains to be seen how well we will pass that test in our generation.

Here, as I see them, are the basic implications of what Joseph Smith taught the Nauvoo Relief Society in 1844:

- **Women may have the priesthood conferred upon them, in our day.**

- **Women may have keys of the kingdom conveyed to them, in our day.**

And at that, all certainty ends. Joseph left us nothing regarding offices or hierarchy, or any of the other thorny questions that would have to be settled to implement the conferral of the priesthood upon women in the 21st century. Apparently it is up to us to seek to the Lord to receive guidance for this. About our current situation, I am reminded of an old New York saying: "You don't ask, you don't get."

There are also some things that we should *not* infer from Joseph's remarks. First of all, we have no record, at least in the *Minute*

Book, that Joseph actually conferred the priesthood on any woman; his statement was a statement of possibility and intent, although the fulfillment of those was cut off by his death and left for our day to fulfill. (So am I saying that Joseph Smith conferred keys of the kingdom on people who did not hold the priesthood at the time? That is not for me to say. But I don't argue with Joseph Smith.)

Secondly, whatever keys of the kingdom may have been conveyed by Joseph to the Relief Society presidency of the time, those keys were nullified when the first Relief Society president, Emma Smith, left the Church. There is certainly no record of Emma passing keys on to anyone else, either. No keys of the kingdom are held by the general Relief Society presidency in our day.

Third, none of what Joseph said means that anyone could choose to simply ordain an LDS woman tomorrow after lunch. There are very active keys of the kingdom in our day, and the entirety of them are held by the President of the Church, who is the only person authorized to change policies like conferring the priesthood upon women.

The priesthood policies of our day could change. But such is the story of Chapter 5 ("The Future").

Why Have We Not Heard About This Before?

I would not be surprised if some readers find themselves wondering, "Why haven't I read or heard about these statements by Joseph Smith before now?" For it is a fact that some of these statements have had no exposure in Church literature from January 1971 through April 2014 (see Table 1-1, pp. 30-31).

As we see in Table 1-1, Joseph Smith has been quoted accurately from the *Nauvoo R. S. Minute Book* as saying "I now turn the key to you" a baker's dozen of times, all dating from 1992 on. He has been quoted inaccurately from George A. Smith's account ("I now turn the key in your behalf") the same number of times, with 10 instances occurring before 1992. I cannot help but think that the reason the accurate words have been quoted from 1992 on is that this was the year that saw the publication of the hardcover edition of a history of Relief Society, *Women of Covenant*, which reports the Prophet's words accurately.[48]

However, the other, even more provocative statements of Joseph Smith—saying that he would make of the Relief Society "a kingdom of priests," and that he would deliver the keys of the kingdom to the Relief Society leadership—have *never* been cited in major Church organs since 1971: they have never been quoted in General Conference, or in a Church magazine, or in a Church-published manual (although they have been reported in *Women of Covenant*). Given the major import of Joseph Smith's sayings, this is quite interesting.

So why are these more provocative statements of Joseph Smith so little known? There are two answers to this question: (1) at one time, at least some Relief Society sisters *had* heard about these statements, but that knowledge was lost as the *Minute Book* became largely inaccessible to the public; and, (3) however unintentionally, the widely available *History of the Church* distorted the accounts of Joseph Smith's teachings to the Nauvoo Relief Society.

At one time, the words of Joseph Smith as given in the *Nauvoo Relief Society Minute Book* were well known to some Relief Society sisters. The original *Minute Book* had been brought across the Great Plains with the Saints by Eliza R. Snow, who later became the second president of the general Relief Society when it was reorganized in 1867 in Utah. Upon her death in 1887, it passed into the hands of Bathsheba W. Smith, the fourth president.

However, for a full century after the death of Sister Smith in 1910, the *Nauvoo Relief Society Minute Book* was available only to scholars who visited the Church History Department in person. As recently as 2005, the *Minute Book* was described by two scholars as "one of the least-tapped sources in the ongoing effort to retrieve the teachings of the Prophet Joseph Smith."[49]

---

[48] Derr, Cannon, & Beecher (1992/2000) pp. 46-47.
[49] Derr & Madsen (2005) p. 123.

	Number of Times Mentioned in		
Joseph Smith teaching	General Conference	*Ensign / New Era*	Manuals
1. "[JS] said he was going to make of this Society a kingdom of priests as in Enoch's day—as in Paul's day" a	0	0	0
2. "[JS] spoke of delivering the keys to this Society and to the church" b	0	0	0
3. "[JS said] that the keys of the kingdom are about to be given to them [the sisters], that they may be able to detect every thing false—as well as to the Elders[.]" c	0	0	0
4. "I now turn the key to you in the name of God" d	6	4	3
-. "I now turn the key in your behalf" e	2	8	3

Notes: Sources enumerated were found through use of the Search function of the Church's website (www.lds.org/search), which contains transcripts of General Conference talks (April 1971 through April 2014), Church magazines (January 1971 through April 2014), and Church manuals (generally, 1971 through April 2014). Figures for the *Ensign* do not include General Conference talks.

[a] Joseph Smith, in *Nauvoo Relief Society Minute Book*, p. 22.
[b] Joseph Smith, in *Nauvoo Relief Society Minute Book*, p. 37.
[c] Joseph Smith, in *Nauvoo Relief Society Minute Book*, p. 38.
[d] Joseph Smith, in *Nauvoo Relief Society Minute Book*, p. 40.
[e] George A. Smith's rewriting of Joseph Smith's words, *History, 1838-1856, Volume C-1 Addenda* (1854) p. 41-42; *History of the Church* (1908), vol. 4, p. 607; *Teachings of the Prophet Joseph Smith* (J. F. Smith, 1938) pp. 238-239.

Table 1-1. Frequency with which key phrases from Joseph Smith's 1842 remarks appear on the Church website.

The *Minute Book* has become available to the general public through the Joseph Smith Papers Project, which has made documents like the *Minute Book* available online in original manuscript and in typescript,[50] only since June 5, 2012.[51] So, one reason most readers have not seen these materials is that they have not been released to the public for very long.

Another reason that readers may not be familiar with these statements of Joseph Smith is more troublesome. A great deal of LDS instructional material regarding Church history is based on the seven-volume *History of the Church* (*HC*)—which in some cases is simply not true to original documents, such as the *Nauvoo Relief Society Minute Book*.[52] How this came to be requires some explanation.

It is important for the reader to understand that there are several different layers of documents at work here, all involving different authors, scribes, and editors (see Figure 1-2). These different layers of documents are as follows:

1. **Original documents** from the era of Joseph Smith.[53] These include documents written down by the Prophet himself, or by scribes, secretaries, and even diarists, as the Prophet spoke, or shortly thereafter.

---

[50] http://josephsmithpapers.org/paperSummary/nauvoo-relief-society-minute-book

[51] *2013 Church Almanac* (2012) p. 31, entry for June 5.

[52] The *History of the Church* (1902-1932) was edited by Elder B. H. Roberts, then one of the First Seven Presidents of Seventy. He based what he wrote on manuscripts collectively called "The History of Joseph Smith," or the *Manuscript History of the Church*, much of which had been written by scribes after the Prophet's death (Jessee, 1971; note especially the chart on p. 441).

[53] Many of these are now available at the Joseph Smith Papers Project, http://josephsmithpapers.org/ .

1: What Joseph Smith Said About Women & Priesthood 33

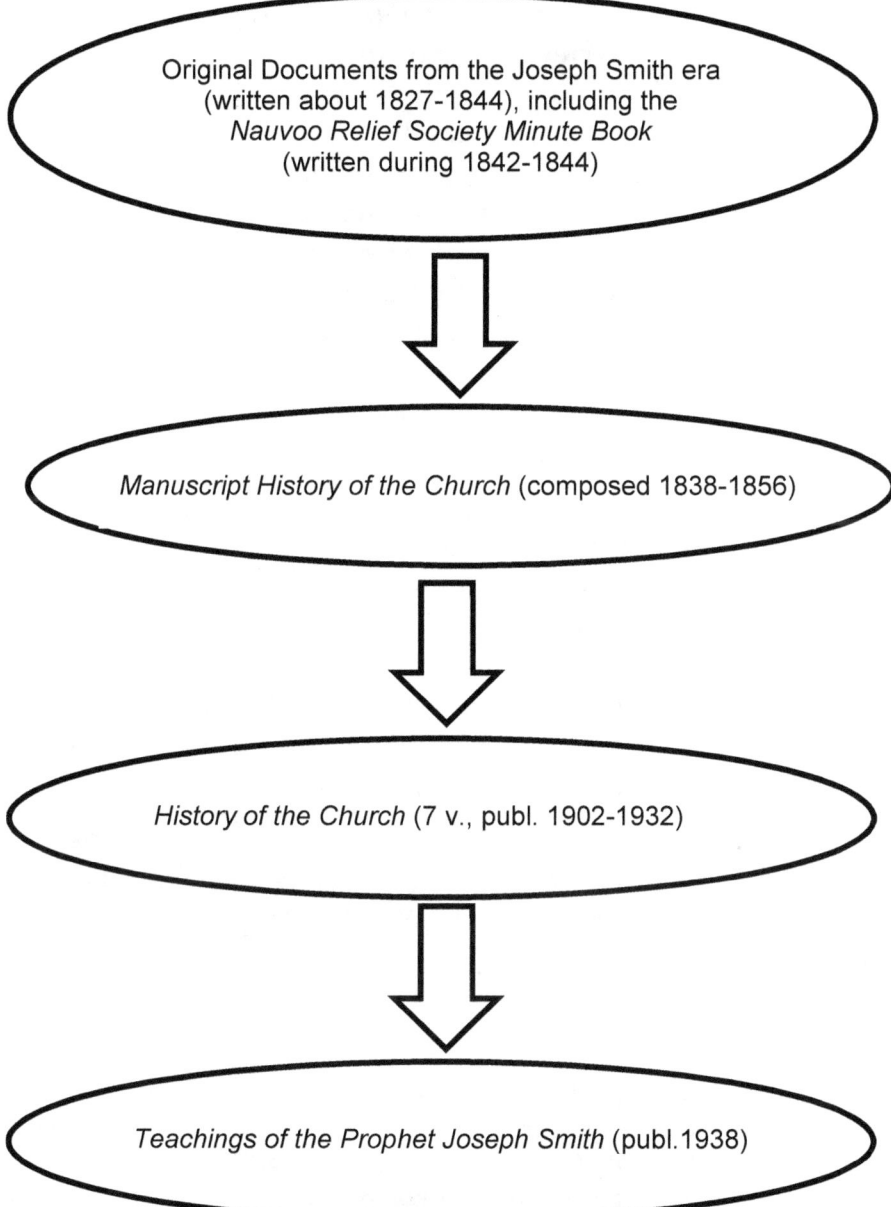

Figure 1-2. Relationships between original documents, *Manuscript History*, and major publications of LDS history.

2. **The *Manuscript History of the Church*,**[54] written by Joseph's secretaries and their successors, often years after Joseph's death.[55] Although written in the first-person voice of the Prophet himself, the content of the Manuscript History often reflects actual *composition* by the various scribes, based on their own understandings, which expand upon—and, sometimes, significantly change—what the Prophet actually said or wrote. This kind of interpretive re-writing of one's original sources—done without any notice given to the reader—was common in the writing of history during the 19th century.[56]

3. **The 7-volume *History of the Church*** edited by B. H. Roberts for the Church.[57] This largely reflects the material in the Manuscript History, as edited and annotated by B. H. Roberts. This publication has been one of the most-often-quoted sources in LDS instructional materials about the Church's history (for example, Sunday School manuals and publications of the Church Educational System).

4. **The one-volume collection, *Teachings of the Prophet Joseph Smith*.**[58] This, too, is often quoted in LDS instructional materials. To a large extent, it is

---

[54] Until recently, the *Manuscript History* was available only to scholars who visited the Church History Department in person. Now, much of the *Manuscript History* is available online, both in images of the original pages, and in typescript, at the Joseph Smith Papers Project: http://josephsmithpapers.org/the-papers#/H2L/JSPPH3

[55] Jessee (1971); see especially the chart on p. 441.

[56] Jessee (1976) pp. 24-27.

[57] *History of the Church* (1902-1932). This is not to be confused with B. H. Roberts own multivolume publication on Church history, known as the *Comprehensive History of the Church*, or *CHC*.

[58] J. F. Smith (1938).

based on the 7-volume *History of the Church*.[59] The *Teachings* volume also makes some use of the *Manuscript History*.

Comparing the teachings of Joseph Smith as recorded in original documents with the way these teachings have been conveyed in the *Manuscript History* can be quite eye-opening. For example:

From the *Nauvoo Relief Society Minute Book* (30 March 1842):

> [President Joseph Smith said] ... all must act in concert or nothing can be done—that **the Society should move according to the ancient Priesthood**, hence there should be **a select Society** separate from all the evils of the world, choice, virtuous and holy— **Said he was going to make of this Society a kingdom of priests** as in Enoch's day—as in Pauls day—that it is the privilege of each member to live long and enjoy health—....[60]

From the *Manuscript History* under this date:

> [President Joseph Smith said:] ... all must act in concert, or nothing can be done—and should move according to the Ancient Priesthood; hence **the Saints should be a select people**, separate from all the evils of the world, choice, virtuous and holy—**the Lord was going to make of the Church of Jesus Christ a kingdom of Priests, a holy people,** a chosen generation, as in Enoch's day, having all the gifts "as illustrated to the Church in Paul's epistles and teachings

---

[59] The *Teachings* volume refers to the *History of the Church* by the abbreviation "D.H.C.," standing for "Documentary History of the Church," a now-outdated name for that collection.

[60] *Nauvoo Relief Society Minute Book* (1842-1844) p. 22-23, emphases added. The secretary who took these minutes is recorded as Eliza R. Snow (p. 25).

to the Churches in his day—that it is the privilege of each member to live long, and enjoy health. He then blessed the Saints[.]"[61]

The *Manuscript History* version was composed in 1854, ten years after the Prophet's death.[62] It is obvious that the content of the *Manuscript History* version is different from that of the *R.S. Minute Book*, the original document involved. The *Manuscript History* substitutes "the Saints" or the Church itself for the Relief Society. These are crucially important changes that alter the entire meaning of Joseph Smith's remarks—and effectively disenfranchise the Relief Society, who in the *Manuscript History* version no longer are going to be made into a kingdom of priests. In essence, the *Manuscript History* version is a retcon, reworking Joseph's words in the past to fit the practice of the Church in the scribe's present.

The 7-volume *History of the Church* presents the inaccurate account of Joseph Smith's remarks as given in the *Manuscript History* essentially verbatim, with minor changes in punctuation.[63] In turn, the inaccurate rendering in the *History of the Church* was excerpted for the very popular work *Teachings of the Prophet Joseph Smith*.[64] Of course, both the *History of the Church* and *Teachings of the Prophet Joseph Smith* have been cited widely in Church instructional materials.

Another example: From the *Nauvoo Relief Society Minute Book* under date of 28 April 1842, reporting the Prophet Joseph's talk:

> **He spoke of delivering the keys to this Society and to the church**—that according to his prayers God had appointed him elsewhere[.][65]

---

[61] *History, 1838-1856, Volume C-1 Addenda* (1854) p. 62, emphases added.
[62] "Source note" to the online version of *History, 1838-1856, Volume C-1 Addenda* (1854).
[63] *History of the Church* (1908) vol. 4, p. 570.
[64] J. F. Smith (1938) pp. 201-202.
[65] *Nauvoo Relief Society Minute Book* (1842-1844) p. 37, emphases added.

1: What Joseph Smith Said About Women & Priesthood

From the *Manuscript History* under this date:

> **He spoke of delivering the keys of the Priesthood to the church**, and said that **the faithful members of the Relief Society should receive them in connection with their husbands** that the Saints whose integrity has been tried and proved faithful might know how to ask the Lord and receive an answer; for according to his [blank] prayers God had appointed him elsewhere.[66]

Here, again, the account in the *Manuscript History* changed the entire meaning of Joseph Smith's statement as given in the *R.S. Minute Book*, and took the keys out of the hands of the Relief Society, as it were. Much wording is added that is not included in the Prophet's remarks at all, some of it quite prejudicial to the matter of women and the priesthood. It is a retcon, pure and simple. As in my earlier example, the inaccurate *Manuscript History* version of the Prophet's discourse was preserved in the *History of the Church*[67]; in turn this inaccurate *HC* version has been perpetuated in *Teachings of the Prophet Joseph Smith*.[68]

A final example from this same discourse will do. In this case, the inaccurate version of the Prophet's remarks has been quoted far and wide in LDS periodicals and instructional materials.

From the *Nauvoo Relief Society Minute Book* (28 April 1842):

> This Society is to get instruction thro' the order which God has established—thro' the medium of those appointed to lead—and **I now turn the key to you** in the name of God and this Society shall rejoice and knowledge and intelligence shall flow down

---

[66] *History, 1838-1856, Volume C-1 Addenda* (1854) p. 39, emphases added.
[67] *History of the Church* (1908), vol. 4, p. 604, emphasis added.
[68] J. F. Smith (1938) p. 226.

from this time—this is the **beginning of better days, to this Society[.]**[69]

From the *Manuscript History* under this date:

[Y]ou will receive instruction through the order of the Priesthood which God has established, through the medium of those appointed to lead guide and direct the affairs of the church in this last Dispensation and **I now turn the key in your behalf** in the name of the Lord, and this society shall rejoice and knowledge and intelligence shall flow down from this time henceforth; **this is the beginning of better days to the poor and needy**, who shall be made to rejoice and pour forth blessings on your heads.[70]

What we see here—yet another retcon, indeed—is a subtle but important change in wording. In the *Relief Society Minute Book*, the Prophet Joseph says that he "turns the key *to you*." This is changed in the version recorded in the *Manuscript History*, which has Joseph instead *exercising* priesthood keys rather than *passing* them ("I now turn the key in your behalf"). In addition, the *R.S. Minute Book* account follows up the passage involving the key with the statement that "this is the beginning of better days, to this Society"—just the sort of thing that would follow *either* the bestowal or turning of priesthood keys; however, the *Manuscript History* account changes the meaning of Joseph's statement entirely, ushering in better days for the poor and needy alone.

At this point, the reader may not be surprised to learn that the inaccurate *Manuscript History* version of the Prophet's remarks became embodied in the *History of the Church*,[71] whence it has been widely quoted in Church literature. Of course, the book *Teachings of*

---

[69] *Nauvoo Relief Society Minute Book* (1842-1844) p. 40, emphasis added.
[70] *History, 1838-1856, Volume C-1 Addenda* (1854) p. 41-42, emphases added.
[71] *History of the Church* (1908), vol. 4, p. 607.

the Prophet Joseph Smith follows the inaccurate account in the *History of the Church*.[72]

One might wonder, who ultimately was responsible for changing the meaning of Joseph Smith's statements, between the time that Eliza R. Snow penned the minutes in the *Nauvoo Relief Society Minute Book* in 1842, and the time that the portion of the *Manuscript History* devoted to these discourses was composed in 1854? The hand likely was that of George A. Smith, then a member of the Quorum of the Twelve, "who, in 1854, was assigned to complete Joseph's history."[73]

I certainly do not think that Elder George A. Smith was up to anything nefarious. He was reconstructing Joseph Smith's remarks according to his own preconceptions of what the Prophet could have meant. This is how people wrote history in mid-19th century America.[74] Unfortunately, the inaccurate writing of LDS history in the mid-19th century has had weighty ramifications right up to the early 21st century.

The Standard Works and Modern Revelation

It is one thing to say that Joseph Smith said these things. It is another to say what they mean.

Is it not possible that I have just given some sort of misbegotten, off-ramp interpretation to Joseph Smith's remarks? If that is so, then likely this would be revealed through an investigation of the Standard Works and the words of the modern prophets when acting as such. That is the journey we enter upon in the next two chapters.

---

[72] J. F. Smith (1938) pp. 238-239.
[73] Newell (1985) p. 22.
[74] Jessee (1976).

2

Justifications for Restricting LDS Priesthood to Men

In this chapter, I consider the justifications that people have offered for restricting LDS ordination to men. (These are not identical to the objections that some have made against the potential ordination of LDS women, which I treat in the following chapter.)

One commonly cited reason for restricting the priesthood to men is the idea that the Lord Himself set up this restriction. However, this is a particularly weak argument, for one simple reason:

> There exists <u>no direct statement</u>, in either the ancient
> or the modern scriptures of the LDS Standard Works,
> or elsewhere in modern revelation, to the effect that
> the Priesthood is to be extended only to men.

Current statements made by Church members simply reiterate words to the effect that 'the Lord made it so,' as if there were some prior statement in the Standard Works to which the Church member is appealing. But there's the rub: there simply *is* no such prior statement in the Standard Works.[75]

Think about that. The Latter-day Saints have, in addition to the Bible, over 900 pages of specifically LDS scriptures in their Standard Works.[76] These specifically LDS scriptures amount to over 75% of

---

[75] I am not the first person to have noticed this. Many have noted that "the scriptures never explicitly state that women may be permitted to hold priesthood or are prohibited from doing so" (Charles, 1985, p. 15).

[76] This includes, in the 1981 edition, 531 pages in the Book of Mormon, 294 pages in the Doctrine and Covenants, 61 pages in the Pearl of

the length of the Old Testament, and over twice the entire length of the New Testament. If the Lord had wanted the Melchizedek Priesthood restricted to men, He had ample room in which to make this explicitly clear in latter-day scripture—not to mention, He has stated nothing in the Bible either. The fact that He did *not* made this explicitly clear in the Standard Works is, at the very least, extremely suggestive.

If the Lord truly meant the Melchizedek Priesthood to only be available to men, why would He not have stated that, explicitly? One single, brief verse of scripture would have done the job. Only five words in the English translation of the Bible were needed to make clear that "Thou shalt not commit adultery,"[77] and that set the doctrine quite clearly for millennia. Simply saying somewhere— almost *anywhere* in the Standard Works—something so simple as "Thou shalt ordain only men" would settle the matter.

It is not as if this were some small issue. The Melchizedek Priesthood is required to perform important ordinances, some with eternal consequences. These days, the Saints often hear statements to the effect that "Woman is an equal partner with her husband in the Melchizedek Priesthood"[78]; whatever that actually means, it certainly does *not* mean that women can perform these ordinances, nor can they serve in the governing quorums of the Church.[79]

Look at it this way. As the scriptures record it, the course of one of the most important civilizations known to humankind was set, in part, by the ruler's desire for a priesthood that he could not hold.[80]

Great Price, and 17 pages of excerpts from the Joseph Smith Translation (beyond footnotes) in the 1979 LDS edition of the Bible: 903 pages.

[77] Exodus 20:14. In the Hebrew, this only takes two words, one of which means "Don't!"; *JPS Hebrew-English Tanakh* (1999) p. 156, Exodus 20:13.

[78] Olson (2011b) p. 662.

[79] The exception, of course, is that women administer certain ordinances to women in LDS temples. Of course, this raises questions all by itself: If women can perform *some* ordinances, then why not all?

[80] I refer, of course, to ancient Egypt, sometime before 2000 BC, and one of the early Pharaohs; see The Pearl of Great Price, Abraham 1:26-27.

2: Justifications for Restricting LDS Priesthood to Men

To put it in the vernacular, holding the Priesthood is a very big deal indeed.

Instead of scripture, there are two sorts of support given for the assertion that "the Lord restricted the priesthood to men." One is a set of arguments of the form "it *is* this way because it *ought* to be this way." At best, these are ad hoc, more or less emotional arguments; at worst, these appear to show the kind of logical error that logicians call *the naturalistic fallacy*, the idea that the current state of affairs is somehow a reflection of the natural order of things.[81] In any case, these arguments are, at heart, simply people's opinions, and as I said in the Preface, when it comes to such an important subject I am not interested in people's opinions, regardless of who those people are. Questions about something so crucial as the priesthood should not be settled by mortal opinions.

There is another sort of support for the assertion that "the Lord restricted the priesthood to men." It points to the scriptural record, which does not record the ordination of women to priesthood offices. Below, I consider various eras of scriptural history to explore this matter.

"The ancient Melchizedek Priesthood was only given to men."

One might point out that the ancient Melchizedek Priesthood was only given to men so far as scripture records, and that on this basis, we today ought only to give the priesthood to men. As it happens, this line of reasoning is quite weak, especially when we

---

[81] The term "naturalistic fallacy" has other meanings as well. More precisely, the problem with statements of this type, "it *is* this way because it *ought* to be this way," is called by moral philosophers the "is-ought problem." the prime thinker here has been the 18th century philosopher David Hume, who essentially stated that there is no logical connection between what *is* and what *ought* to be. This severing between *is* and *ought* is called Hume's Law, or, more colorfully, Hume's Guillotine.

consider the circumstances in which Gospel-believing families found themselves in the ancient world.

We know very little about the circumstances of the Melchizedek Priesthood before the time of Abraham. Given the sparseness of that record, let us just consider here the history of the Melchizedek Priesthood from the era of Abraham until that of Moses and the Exodus, at which time the Melchizedek Priesthood was withdrawn from among the people of Israel generally. During this period of about five centuries (approximately 1996 BC—1491 BC), certainly there is no scriptural record of a woman having received the Melchizedek Priesthood. But let us look at the context of that situation.

It is beyond dispute that, in ancient times, several non-Abrahamic religions featured females who held these religions' versions of priesthood: simply put, these religions had priestesses. In some of these religions, priestesses engaged in ritual sex with men not their husbands:

- In ancient Sumer (the founding of which predated Abraham's day), the high priestess, called the "Entu," had ritual sexual intercourse with the high priest or king. This happened as part of the "sacred marriage" (*hieros gamos*) ceremony, performed during the New Year festival. This ceremony re-enacted the mythic sexual love of the goddess Inanna and her consort Dumuzi (Dimmuzi).[82]

- During Abraham's life, the *hieros gamos* ceremony was widespread in the Babylonian empire, with the goddess Ishtar taking the place of Inanna, and her consort Tammuz the place of Dumuzi. Ishtar was served by priestesses known as *ishtaritu* or "Joy-Maidens," who used sexual rituals in their temples. "In many temples, the priestesses would undertake the sacred marriage with any male worshipper who wanted union with the god-

---

[82] Dening (1996) pp. 48-49.

dess. The man, whom the priestess had not met before and would not meet again, spent the night with her in the temple precincts."[83]

- Across the span of at least 14 centuries, from the days of ancient Sumer (pre-Abraham) right through the days of the prophet Jeremiah (about 620 BC), the goddess Asherah was worshipped in the Near East and Middle East—including sometimes in the land of Israel, and sometimes by the Israelites themselves (often the cause of prophetic condemnation). Some have associated with Asherah the devotion of a type of women known in Hebrew as a *qideshah* (קְדֵשָׁה). This word comes from the same root (קד״ש, Q-D-Sh)[84] used in the words *qodesh* (קֹדֶשׁ),[85] meaning "holiness," and *qadosh* (or *kadosh*, קָדוֹשׁ),[86] meaning "holy," originally from the idea of being set aside, dedicated, or even consecrated.[87] However, a *qideshah* was 'consecrated' to sexual activity, in connection with a non-Israelite temple,[88] often in the service of the pagan goddess Asherah. (The term is thus translated as "whore" or "harlot" in the King James Version of the Bible,[89] even though there is a different Hebrew word used in the Bible for "prostitute"; Jewish translations of the Bible into English might use the term

---

[83] Dening (1996) p. 56; see pp. 54-57.
[84] F. Brown, Driver, & Briggs (1906/1951), p. 871, entry for root קד״ש.
[85] F. Brown, Driver, & Briggs (1906/1951), p. 871, entry for word קֹדֶשׁ.
[86] F. Brown, Driver, & Briggs (1906/1951), p. 872, entry for word קָדוֹשׁ.
[87] F. Brown, Driver, & Briggs (1906/1951), p. 871, entry for root קדש.
[88] F. Brown, Driver, & Briggs (1906/1951), p. 873, entry for word קָדֵשׁ, "temple-prostitute," subentry for "קְדֵשָׁה (woman)."
[89] The term is translated as "harlot" in Gen. 38:21-22 and Hosea 4:14, and as "whore" in Deut. 23:17.

"cult prostitute" for *qideshah*.[90]) In their sexual activity, these women essentially functioned as a type of priestess in an apostate religion of the day.

The conclusion is clear: the association between priestesses and a type of sexuality that was illicit (from a Gospel perspective) was very strong in the ancient world of the Near and Middle East. In this context, ordaining a Gospel-believing woman to the Priesthood would target her for all sorts of unwarranted expectations on the part of adherents of neighboring religions—expectations that would not necessarily be attached to a male priest.

Another way of putting this is that the ancient Near and Middle Eastern societies from Abraham to Moses were unprepared to deal with priestesses who embodied what the Gospel would consider sexual purity and virtue. Ordaining women to the Priesthood in such societies could have endangered the lives of the women involved, if non-Gospel-believers attempted to obtain the sexual favors that priestesses in some of the neighboring religions provided.

In this light, the absence of a scriptural record for women's ordination between the ages of Abraham and Moses does *not* mean that the Priesthood is meant inherently to be restricted to men. Rather, the societies in which Gospel-believing people were imbedded would have posed a danger to Gospel-oriented priestesses.

"The ancient Aaronic Priesthood was only given to men."

Of course, one could easily point out that from the time that Moses instituted the Aaronic Priesthood (about 1491 BC), this too was only given to men. There are those who would take this as evidence that the higher or Melchizedek Priesthood should only be extended to men. However, this proposition rests on very shaky

---

[90] See the *JPS Hebrew-English Tanakh* (1999) translations for Gen. 38:21, Deut. 23:18.

2: Justifications for Restricting LDS Priesthood to Men 47

foundations indeed. To understand how this is so, it will be useful to understand how the Aaronic Priesthood came to be.

The Aaronic Priesthood was given to the people Israel as part of the Mosaic Law, during the exodus from Egypt. After Moses led the people out of Egypt, and camped them at the foot of Mt. Sinai, Moses went up into the mountain and communed with the Lord.[91] After receiving the teachings of the Ten Commandments,[92] Moses looked in on the Israelites, who were utterly terrified at the smoke, fire, and thunderings that they witnessed occurring on Mt. Sinai.[93] Moses reassured them,[94] then returned to the mount and received more law from the Lord.[95]

Moses returned to the Israelites and read them the law, which the people accepted by covenant.[96] Moses then returned to the mount at the Lord's command to receive the law on stone tablets,[97] including other ordinances (much of which dealt with the tabernacle that the Lord wished to be built).[98] Moses received two stone tablets of the law written by the finger of the Lord, outlining these laws and ordinances for the people.[99]

The Israelites, being impatient with Moses' long absence (forty days and nights), commanded Aaron to build for them an idol to worship and to go before them (presumably planning to resume their journey to the Promised Land); this was the famous golden calf incident.[100] Upon his return to the Israelites' camp, and angry at

---

[91] Exodus chapter 19.
[92] Exodus 20:1-17,
[93] Exodus 20:18-19, 21.
[94] Exodus: 20:20.
[95] Exodus:20:22-26; Exodus chapters 21-23.
[96] Exodus 24:1-8.
[97] Exodus 24:12-13.
[98] Exodus chapters 25-31.
[99] Exodus 31:18.
[100] Exodus chapter 32.

seeing their idolatrous sin, Moses broke the two stone tablets he had received from the Lord.[101]

Moses imposed severe discipline among the Israelites (including the execution of three thousand Israelite men[102]). Moses then received a command of the Lord:

> And the Lord said unto Moses, Hew thee two other tables of stone, like unto the first, and I will write upon them also, the words of the law, according as they were written at the first on the tables which thou breakest; but it shall not be according to the first, for I will take away the priesthood[103] out of their midst; therefore, my holy order, and the ordinances thereof, shall not go before them; for my presence shall not go up in their midst, lest I destroy them.
>
> But I will give unto them the law as at the first, but it shall be after the law of a carnal commandment; for I have sworn in my wrath, that they shall not enter into my presence, into my rest, in the days of their pilgrimage. Therefore do as I have commanded thee, and be ready in the morning, and come up in the morning unto mount Sinai, and present thyself there to me in the top of the mount.[104]

Moses was with the Lord on the top of Mount Sinai again for another forty days and nights. He returned with the law of God on the second set of tablets.[105] But what these tablets lacked, as indicat-

---

[101] Exodus 32:19.
[102] Exodus 32:26-28.
[103] That is, the Melchizedek Priesthood.
[104] Joseph Smith Translation, Exodus 34:1-2. (Found in the 1979 Latter-day Saint edition of the Holy Bible, Appendix p. 800.)
[105] Exodus 34:28-29.

2: Justifications for Restricting LDS Priesthood to Men 49

ed in the portion just quoted, were instructions regarding the Melchizedek or Higher Priesthood.

What Moses had on the second set of stone tables was a complex system of rules and requirements.[106] The Latter-day Saints, along with many other Christians, and many Jews, call this system the Mosaic Law. It encompassed not just what was on the stone tablets, but many subsequent rules given during the time of Moses' ministry (for example, see the entire book of Leviticus).

Christians have long taught that the Mosaic Law was a "schoolteacher" of sorts, to prepare a people to receive Jesus as the Messiah. As the apostle Paul wrote, "Wherefore then serveth the law? It was added because of transgressions …."[107]

I have given all this background to make it clear that arguments about this or that LDS practice that are based on appeals to the Mosaic Law are on extremely shaky ground. The Ten Commandments themselves[108] — which Moses received on the very first of his several trips to the summit of Mt. Sinai, before the stone tablets were even issued[109] — are not part of the Mosaic Law, but are part of eternal Gospel law.[110] However *nothing* in the Mosaic Law—including the

---

[106] See Exodus, chapters 20-23, 25-31.
[107] Galatians 3:19.
[108] Exodus 20:1-17.
[109] Exodus chapter 19; 20:18-22.
[110] Elder Jos. Fielding Smith, then of the Quorum of the Twelve, wrote:
> Some people have the idea that the Ten Commandments … were first given by Moses when he directed the children of Israel and formulated their code of laws. This is not the case. These great commandments are from the beginning and were understood in righteous communities in the days of Adam. They are, in fact, fundamental parts of the Gospel of Jesus Christ, and the Gospel in its fulness was first given to Adam. (Joseph Fielding Smith, 1941, p. 525; excerpted in Joseph Fielding Smith, 1954-1956, Vol. 1, p. 96)

This seems to be the normative opinion among LDS scholars today (e.g., Olson, 2011a).

arrangements regarding the Aaronic Priesthood—applies to people of our day, Latter-day Saint or not. As the Apostle Paul put it:

> Wherefore the law was our schoolmaster to bring us unto Christ, that we might be justified by faith.
>
> But after that faith is come, we are no longer under a schoolmaster.
>
> For ye are all the children of God by faith in Christ Jesus.
>
> For as many of you as have been baptized into Christ have put on Christ.
>
> There is neither Jew nor Greek, there is neither bond nor free, there is neither male nor female: for ye are all one in Christ Jesus.
>
> And if ye be Christ's then are ye Abraham's seed, and heirs according to the promise.[111]

There is much that could be said about this passage. The most important concept for the moment, however, is to underline the idea that the Mosaic Law is no longer applicable. As Jesus said to the Book of Mormon peoples after His resurrection: "... by me redemption cometh, and in me is the law of Moses fulfilled."[112]

Of course, there are many provisions of the Mosaic Law that would result in arrest, lengthy imprisonment, and perhaps capital punishment *for the enforcers* of the Law, if these provisions were followed today. For example:

- "And he that smiteth his father, or his mother, shall surely be put to death" (Ex. 21:15).

- "And he that curseth his father, or his mother, shall surely be put to death" (Ex. 21:17; see also Lev. 20:9).

- A thief could be sold into slavery (Ex. 22:3).

---

[111] Galatians 3:24-29.
[112] 3 Nephi 9:17.

- "He that sacrificeth unto any god, save unto the Lord only, he shall be utterly destroyed" (Ex. 22:20).

- "Ye shall keep the sabbath therefore; for it is holy unto you: every one that defileth it shall surely be put to death" (Ex. 31:14; see also Ex. 35:2 and Lev. 23:30).

- Adultery was punishable by the death of both parties (Lev. 20:10; see also Deut. 22:22).

- A prostitute who was the daughter of a priest was to be burned to death (Lev. 21:9).

- One who blasphemed the name of the Lord and cursed was to be put to death (Lev. 24:16).

- Those who worshipped false gods were to be stoned to death (Deut. 17:2-5).

- A "stubborn and rebellious son" was to be brought by his parents before the elders of his city and accused; then the men of the city were to stone the son to death (Deut. 21: 18-21).

- A woman whom the elders of the city determined had not been a virgin when she married was to be stoned to death (Deut. 22:13-21).

I personally oppose each of the offenses mentioned above; I'm certainly not in favor of adultery, blasphemy, idolatry, prostitution, Sabbath-breaking, or so forth. But in the 21st century, even in only nominally Christian nations, there would (and should!) be international outcry if the death penalty were applied for these offenses.

As Latter-day Saints, along with many other Christians, we understand that these rules had a point for ancient Israel, to teach principles of holiness—literally, "separation" from the world and dedication to the Lord. But we also understand that these commandments for the execution of certain offenders are no longer to be followed.

But, as with some of the Mosaic Law, so with all. One cannot justify any practice today based on any statute of the Mosaic Law. Here too, those who claim that only men should have the priesthood today because only men held the Aaronic Priesthood anciently find themselves building their argument upon foundations of sand.

"Jesus only ordained men as his apostles."

For many people, it seems that the most important evidence that the Melchizedek Priesthood is to be a male-only domain is the fact that the scriptures record Jesus ordaining only men as apostles. However, this is an extremely weak argument, for several reasons.

First of all, this is clearly only indirect evidence. Yes, Jesus ordained only men as his ancient apostles. But *why* did He do this? As I mentioned on the first page of this chapter, there is no direct statement, in the ancient or modern LDS Standard Works, stating that the Melchizedek Priesthood is to be restricted to men.

Second, the context of Jesus' actions strongly suggests that there were cultural factors at work in his decision to only ordain men. I do not mean Jesus' culture; I mean the cultures among whom His apostles soon would be working.

After His resurrection and just before His ascension into heaven, Jesus gave His apostles a direction that for centuries has been called the Great Commission. It is recorded in the final five verses of the testimony of St. Matthew:

> Then the eleven disciples went away into Galilee, into a mountain where Jesus had appointed them.
> And when they saw him, they worshipped him: but some doubted.
> And Jesus came and spake unto them, saying, All power is given unto me in heaven and in earth.

> Go ye therefore and teach all nations, baptizing them in the name of the Father, and of the Son, and of the Holy Ghost:
>
> Teaching them to observe all things whatsoever I have commanded you: and lo, I am with you always, even unto the end of the world. Amen.[113]

But into what sort of world did the Lord sent his Apostles? Almost entirely, it was the world of the Roman Empire—a place that had very specific ideas about women holding authority.

By the conclusion of the history given in the Acts of the Apostles (about 61 AD), the Roman Empire (see Figure 2-1) had encompassed most of the ancient Greek world, and much more besides, stretching from Spain in the west to the farther shores of the Black Sea in the east, including all of North Africa from Egypt to Gibraltar, and north past Londinium (modern London) in what is now England and Wales. Ancient Christian traditions place the tombs of several of the original Apostles at various places around the Empire as it stood in 60 AD: Philip and Bartholomew in Turkey, Andrew in Greece, Peter in Rome, James the son of Zebedee in Spain. Only the tomb of the apostle Thomas is placed by tradition outside the boundaries of the Roman Empire, in India.

After Jesus' resurrection, the surviving original apostles, along with the new apostles Matthias and Paul, preached to many different communities—Jews in Palestine and around the Empire; Greeks in Corinth and elsewhere; Roman gentile citizens in many places—but aside from, perhaps, Thomas, the ministry of these apostles seems to have been entirely within the bounds of the Roman Empire. No doubt there were advantages to this. As one scholar noted:

> Later Christian writers looked back to the origin of the faith and saw the work of divine providence in the coincidence of the birth of Jesus and the reign of

---

[113] Matthew 28:16-20. See also Mark 16:14-15.

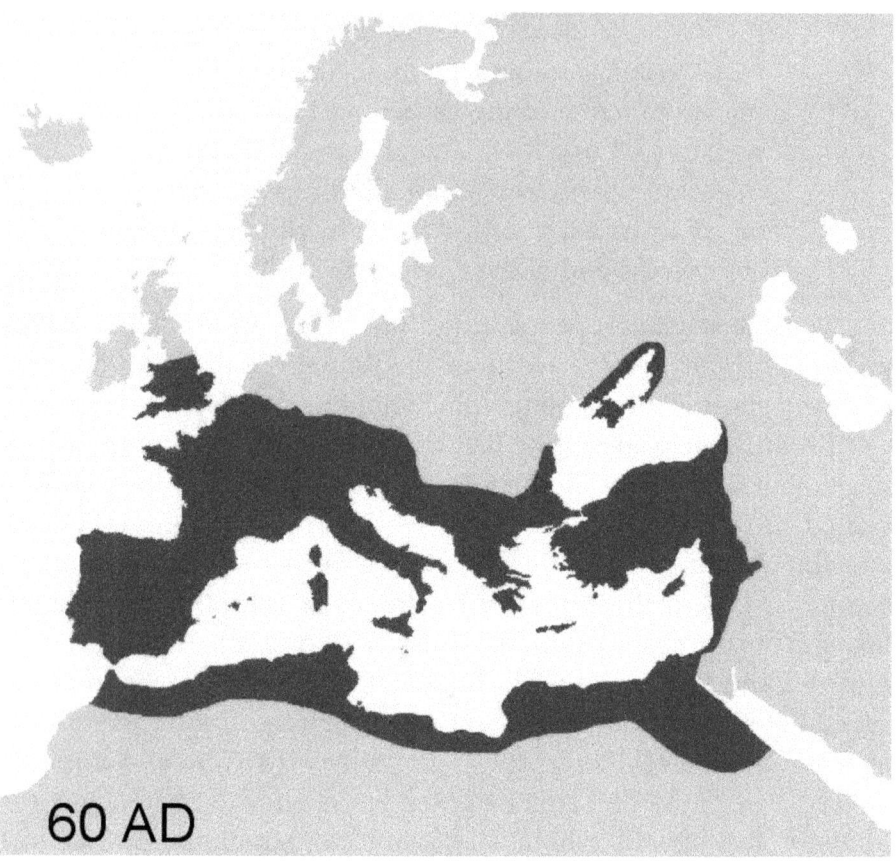

Figure 2-1. The boundaries of the Roman Empire, about 60 AD.

Augustus, the first Roman emperor. Under Augustus and his successors the empire stretched from the northwest corner of Europe to Egypt and from Mauritania to the Black Sea. It brought fifty million or more inhabitants under relatively stable rule—an ideal setting for the growth of a new religion.[114]

However, there were consequences to founding the Christian Church within the Roman Empire. The place of women in the reli-

---

[114] Saller (1993) p. 657.

gious world during the days of the Empire paints an interesting picture of the kind of expectations that Romans would have had of hypothetical clergy who were Christian females.[115]

In the Roman world, women had no official part in public life, being permitted neither to vote nor to hold public office. All women had to be under the legal guardianship of some man (typically her father or husband), regardless of age. (An exception were the priestesses known as the Vestals; see below.)

Among Roman citizens, the male head of the household, the *paterfamilias*, was in charge of maintaining the traditional Roman religious ceremonies of the home. Most priests presiding over the Roman state religion were men. Some types of state priesthood were held by a married couple, who were not permitted to divorce.

Some of the Empire's state religions did have priestesses. The goddess Vesta was served by the College of Vestals, all women. Only six in number, these priestesses were required to abstain from marriage or sexual relations; the violation of this vow was punished by the offending priestess being whipped and then buried alive. The priestesses of the goddess Ceres also seem to have been required to be celibate during the terms of their offices.

The *Bona Dea* ("Good Goddess") was served by the Vestals within the city of Rome, and outside the city by local priestesses. However, from the days of Julius Caesar (1st century BC) through the early 2nd century AD, *Bona Dea*'s festivals were suspected of degenerating into orgies, at least under the local priestesses.

Under these circumstances, ordaining females to the Christian priesthood would have been highly problematic. Roman society was not accustomed to women giving direction (other than to their own workers or slaves). When women did give direction in religious groups, priestesses were often associated with either extended celibacy with abstention from marriage, or orgies, neither of which

---

[115] The following four paragraphs reflect material in Beard et al. (1998), Frier & McGinn (2004), Herbert-Brown (1994), Scheid (2003), and Schultz (2006).

would be appropriate for Gospel-believing people. Indeed, one can easily imagine circumstances where hypothetical Christian priestesses would have been at risk of their lives, either because of their marital relationships (for which Vestals would be tortured and executed) or because their neighbors would expect to be able to take sexual liberties with them.

In this context, Jesus' ordaining of only men to His apostleship—and, in turn, the Apostles' ordaining of only men to the Christian priesthood—can be seen as a way to protect women in an Imperial society that offered holy women little in the way of protection. In essence, the Roman Empire was not sufficiently morally advanced to be able to deal with women holding the Priesthood.

We should note that Jesus did not do much overtly to overturn the social order in the societies in which early Christians found themselves. Neither Jesus nor his apostles preached against slavery, for instance, nor did they challenge the political hegemony of Rome. Similarly, we should not expect that either Jesus or his apostles would choose that place and time to directly challenge the Imperial culture's apostate attitudes towards women and priesthood.

"LDS General Authorities after Joseph Smith have said that it is God's law that only men hold the priesthood."

There have been dozens if not hundreds of occasions, including talks in General Conference, where LDS General Authorities have said that ordination to the priesthood is restricted to men. Some would say that this settles the matter. As it happens, it does not.

The Prophet Joseph recorded an important principle in his journal on 8 February 1843: "'A Prophet is not always a Prophet[,]' only when he is acting as such."[116]

---

[116] Hedges et al. (2011) p. 256. The principle is mentioned in *History of the Church* vol. 5 p. 265, and from there passed to *Teachings of the Prophet Joseph Smith* (J. F. Smith, 1938, p. 278).

Please do not misunderstand me. I often find General Conference addresses to be inspirational sources of the Word of God with a strong resonance for me and my life. However, by this principle taught by the Prophet Joseph, *not everything* said in General Conference is the Word of God. And this is not something established by just this brief statement in Joseph Smith's journal, either. Elder Harold B. Lee, then a member of the Quorum of the Twelve, taught this principle in 1964:

> It is not to be thought that every word spoken by the General Authorities is inspired, or that they are moved upon by the Holy Ghost in everything they read and write. Now you keep that in mind. I don't care what his position is, if he writes something or speaks something that goes beyond anything that you can find in the standard church works, unless that one be the prophet, seer, and revelator—*please note that one exception*—you may immediately say, 'Well, that is his own idea.' And if he says something that contradicts what is found in the standard church works (I think that is why we call them 'standard'—it is the standard measure of all that men teach), you may know by that same token that it is false, regardless of the position of the man who says it.[117]

Pres. Joseph Fielding Smith taught this in his personal correspondence (these excerpts of which were published publicly while he was the President of the Quorum of the Twelve):

> It makes no difference what is written or what *anyone* has said, if what has been said is in *conflict* with what the Lord has revealed, we can set it aside. *My words, and the teachings of any other member of the Church, high*

---

[117] Quoted in *Doctrine and Covenants Student Manual* (2001) p. 144. Emphases in original.

> *or low, if they do not square with the revelations, we need not accept them.* Let us have this matter clear. We have accepted the four *standard works* as the measuring yardsticks, or balances, by which we *measure every man's doctrine.*
>
> *You cannot accept the books written by the authorities of the Church as standards in doctrine, only in so far as they accord with the revealed word in the standard works.*
>
> Every man who writes is responsible, not the Church, for what he writes. If Joseph Fielding Smith writes something which is out of harmony with the revelations, then every member of the Church is duty bound to reject it. If he writes that which is in perfect harmony with the revealed word of the Lord, then it should be accepted.[118]

In this context, I am reminded of a principle taught during the October 2013 General Conference of the Church by President Dieter F. Uchtdorf, second counselor in the First Presidency:

> We openly acknowledge that in nearly 200 years of Church history—along with an uninterrupted line of inspired, honorable, and divine events—there have been some things said and done that could cause people to question. ...
>
> And, to be perfectly frank, there have been times when members or leaders in the Church have simply made mistakes. There may have been things said or done that were not in harmony with our values, principles, or doctrine.
>
> I suppose the Church would be perfect only if it were run by perfect beings. God is perfect, and His doctrine is pure. But He works through us—His im-

---

[118] Joseph Fielding Smith (1954-1956) vol. 3, pp. 203-204. Emphases in original.

> perfect children—and imperfect people make mistakes. …
>
> This is the way it has always been and will be until the perfect day when Christ Himself reigns personally upon the earth.
>
> It is unfortunate that some have stumbled because of mistakes made by men. But in spite of this, the eternal truth of the restored gospel found in The Church of Jesus Christ of Latter-day Saints is not tarnished, diminished, or destroyed.[119]

Examples could be multiplied.

One of the things that I find most interesting about the many statements made by various Church members to the effect that only men may be ordained to the priesthood is that not once—not *once*—have I heard any of them cite even a single verse of scripture to support their position, nor have I ever heard them cite an unequivocal, "thus-saith-the-Lord"-type revelation. Nor have I heard or read anything by the President of the Church—the only person empowered to receive revelation for the Church—suggesting that the Lord has revealed anything specifically on this matter. I have heard many people in the Church say that the priesthood being restricted to men is 'the Lord's way'; I have not heard the slightest evidence, other than precedent from earlier ages of Gospel history, which some have transformed into some kind of divinely ordained template or such. But such it is not. Precedent informs the decisions made in courts of law; however, the Church is much more than a court of law, and the whole point of revelation is to teach us things that may well break with precedent.

If important statements are being made by Church members without any clear scriptural or revelatory evidence being cited, I can only conclude that there *is* no such evidence to cite. What we have instead are opinions, maybe traditions—but of men, not of God.

---

[119] Uchtdorf (2013) pp. 22-23.

Summary

I began this chapter by claiming that there exists no direct statement, in either the ancient or modern scriptures of the LDS Standard Works, or elsewhere in modern revelation, to the effect that the Priesthood is to be extended only to men. To investigate my own claim, I have considered the scriptural and cultural record for the eras of the biblical patriarchs, the Israelites under the Law of Moses, and the time of Jesus' mortal ministry; I have found not one shred of scriptural evidence supporting the idea that the priesthood should be restricted to men, although I have found plenty of historical evidence that it might have been quite detrimental, even dangerous, for Gospel-believing women to be ordained to the priesthood during these periods.

With reference to the years following Joseph Smith, although we Saints have all heard a great number of times that the priesthood is restricted to men as part of a practice set by the Lord, I have never heard or read anyone either adduce scriptural evidence or proclaim new revelation for that position. Based on the evidence before me, I conclude that my initial claim is correct: there *is* no evidence in the Standard Works or in revelations given to the Church that restricts the priesthood to men.

However, just saying that there is no scriptural reason to restrict the priesthood *to men* does not cover the entire ground of the issue. In Chapter 2, I explore the topic, are there scriptural reasons to ban the priesthood *from women?*

3

Objections to Conferring Priesthood on LDS Women

In this chapter, I consider objections that people might make against the idea of extending LDS ordination to women.

"The Apostle Paul insisted that church authority not be vested in the hands of women."

The ancient Apostle Paul taught this to the Corinthian Saints:

> Let your women keep silence in the churches: for it is not permitted unto them to speak [JST rule]; but they are commanded to be under obedience, as also saith the law.
> And if they will learn any thing, let them ask their husbands at home: for it is a shame for women to speak [JST rule] in the church.[120]

Different lessons can be taken from this scripture. For example, one LDS author has written in relation to part of this passage:

> Latter-day Saints ... are not confused by the apostle Paul's writings to the Corinthian Saints .... Latter-day Saint women are not ordained to "rule," or ad-

---

[120] 1 Corinthians 14:34-35. (Changes in the Joseph Smith Translation [JST] are found in the footnotes to the 1979 LDS edition of the Holy Bible.)

minister ordinances and preside as priesthood leaders in the Church ....[121]

Others take a different approach to Paul's writings about women. For example, Elder Joseph Fielding Smith, then a member of the Quorum of the Twelve, stated the following at the Officers Meeting at the Relief Society General Conference held on October 8, 1958[122]:

> Now, today, we live in a different age, a wonderful age in the restoration of the gospel. As far as I know, in former years or former dispensations of the gospel, our sisters were not called upon to do very much. Even in the days of Paul, they were counseled to be silent in churches and other restrictions were placed upon them. But that was not necessarily in accord with the plan of salvation. The plan of salvation had nothing to do with those restrictions. They were due to the prevailing conditions among the peoples, the customs of the times. ...
>
> ... I have often thought in reading our scriptures, the old scriptures, of the restrictions, apparently, that were placed upon women which the Lord in his wisdom in the dispensation of the fulness of times removed.[123]

Thus, Elder Joseph Fielding Smith is on the record in calling Paul's counsel here something due to cultural conditions prevalent at the time. True, he referred to the King James Translation of the Bible rather than the Joseph Smith Translation, but given his famous erudition in the LDS scriptures and Mormon history, I doubt that this was because Elder Smith was somehow unaware of the differences between KJV and JST in this passage.

---

[121] Olson (2011b) p. 663

[122] Not 1858, as is mistakenly printed in the published account.

[123] Joseph Fielding Smith (1959) p. 5.

I find it of interest that Paul gives no scriptural authority and claims no revelation for the notion that women should not speak/rule in the church. Paul was certainly not shy about quoting scripture to support his ideas; in the letters ascribed to Paul in the New Testament, the author quotes or alludes to passages in the Old Testament on 136 occasions.[124] Nor does Paul quote a revelation to the prophets of his day (such as Peter) restricting the priesthood from women.

Given this situation, it is more than plausible that what Paul said to the Corinthians about women speaking, or even ruling, in church seems to be much like his advice that women must pray with their heads covered[125]—that is, it is advice meant for a specific group of people at a specific time.

"General authorities have explicitly stated that the priesthood is not the domain of women."

Some readers might point to the occasions where General Authorities of the Church in our day have explicitly stated that the priesthood is not the domain of women, or that women are not to be ordained to priesthood offices, or so forth. There are three approaches that I would take in responding to this.

First, I would refer such readers to what I wrote near the conclusion of the preceding chapter, where I addressed the claim that "LDS General Authorities since Joseph Smith have said that it is God's law that only men hold the priesthood." I cited teachings of the Prophet Joseph Smith, President Joseph Fielding Smith, and Elder Harold B. Lee to the effect that not everything said, written, or taught by a General Authority is inspired. The same considerations apply here.

---

[124] Calculated from data in LDS Bible Dictionary, "Quotations."
[125] 1 Corinthians 11:5.

Second, I would remind the reader that in Chapter 1, I cite teachings of the Prophet that showed him to be more than friendly to the idea of women holding the priesthood.

Third, I would point out that President Gordon B. Hinckley himself, during his tenure as President of the Church, stated quite bluntly that the priesthood in the pre-millennial future could be extended to women, through revelation. My guess is that not many of the Saints know this, but the record is clear on this point.

On November 9, 1997, the ABC television network in Australia aired an interview with President Hinckley as part of their news show, "Compass." A portion of the interview ran as follows ("RB" indicates one of the interviewers, and of course "GBH" indicates President Hinckley):

> *RB:* At present women are not allowed to be priests in your Church. Why is that?
>
> *GBH:* That's right, because the Lord has put it that way. ….
>
> *RB:* You say the Lord has put it that way. What do you mean by that?
>
> *GBH:* I mean that's a part of His programme. Of course it is, yes.
>
> *RB:* Is it possible that the rules could change in the future as the rules are on Blacks ?
>
> *GBH:* He could change them yes. If He were to change them that's the only way it would happen.
>
> *RB:* So you'd have to get a revelation?
>
> *GBH:* Yes. But there's no agitation for that. We don't find it. Our women are happy. They're satisfied.

> These bright, able, wonderful women who administer their own organisation are very happy. ....[126]

Yes, President Hinckley stated that "the Lord has put it that way" in terms of women not holding the priesthood. I cannot help but note that not a shred of substantiation is given for that statement; when asked to explain that statement, President Hinckley essentially just repeated himself. However, the more important thing to note is that President Hinckley explicitly stated that this could change through a revelation from the Lord. This certainly implies that there is no inherent reason why women could not receive the priesthood.

Certainly it is the case that other leaders in the Church have mentioned women as at least potential priestesses. For example, John Taylor, then a member of the Quorum of the Twelve, said this to the Saints in the Bowery in Salt Lake City on August 30, 1857:

> What are we engaged in? We are engaged in building up the kingdom of God, and many of you have been ordained by the revelations of the Almighty to hold the power and authority of the Holy Priesthood. Besides this, you have been ordained kings and queens, and priests and priestesses to your Lord; you have been put in possession of principles that all the kings, potentates, and powers upon the earth are entirely ignorant of: they do not understand it; but you have received this from the hands of God."[127]

---

[126] "Compass interview" (1997).

[127] Taylor (1858). A portion is quoted in Taylor (1941/1987) pp. 221-222. There are those who would place this ordination of women mentioned by Elder Taylor somewhere in the far future. I would only point out that Elder Taylor himself did not do that; rather, he explicitly stated that "you *have been* ordained kings and queens, and priests and priestesses to your Lord" (emphasis added).

There is much that could be said about these passages. For the moment, what matters is to point out that these words of President Hinckley and Elder Taylor lend no support to the idea that women may not hold the Priesthood. Rather, these words imply just the opposite.

"*The Family: A Proclamation to the World* explicitly states that men and women have different roles and spheres of responsibility."

On September 23, 1995, President of the Church Gordon B. Hinckley read *The Family: A Proclamation to the World* as a portion of his message at the General Relief Society Meeting. The section of the Proclamation that addresses different gender roles is rather brief, and is quoted here in its entirety:

> By divine design, fathers are to preside over their families in love and righteousness and are responsible to provide the necessities of life and protection for their families. Mothers are primarily responsible for the nurture of their children. In these sacred responsibilities, fathers and mothers are obligated to help one another as equal partners.[128]

There is absolutely nothing here that would disqualify women from holding priesthood, or that restricts priesthood to men. In fact, the word "priesthood" does not occur anywhere in the Proclamation. In sum, there is nothing in *The Family: A Proclamation to the World* that has any bearing on LDS women and priesthood.

"LDS women do not even *want* to be ordained to the Priesthood!"

The first thing that must be said about this notion is that, even if it were 100% true, it would be utterly irrelevant. Our personal

---

[128] The First Presidency et al. (1995).

wants don't really have much weight in the matter, as many Saints could testify in relation to other types of callings. (Consider the case of anyone who's prayed to be sent to Mission X, and is then sent to Mission Y. Consider the case of anyone who has ever had a calling extended to them that does not seem to be an occasion for unfettered joy.) The Lord extends his callings whither He extends them. But I shall treat this objection as it stands, irrelevant as it is—because in addition to being irrelevant, it is highly inaccurate.

Much has been made of a survey of Saints conducted by the Pew Forum in 2011. A writer for the Pew Forum, in an online press release that has received a great deal of coverage, reported this:

> A 2011 Pew Research Center survey found that most U.S. Mormons oppose the idea of female membership in the priesthood....
>
> Fully nine-in-ten Mormon women (90%) say women should not be ordained, compared with 84% of Mormon men. ...
>
> The belief that women should be ordained to the priesthood is held least among those who have the highest levels of religious commitment; just 4% of Mormons in that group say women should be ordained, while 95% say they should not. Even among Mormons with lower levels of religious commitment, however, nearly seven-in-ten (69%) say women should not be eligible for the priesthood.[129]

There is one problem with these statements. None of them is supported in the slightest by the research that the Pew Research Center actually performed. To understand this, we need to look at the question that the Pew Research Center really asked, the meaning of that question within Latter-day Saint culture, and the questions that the Pew Research Center did *not* ask—but should have.

---

[129] Lipka (2013).

The Pew Research Center asked the following questions of those whom it surveyed (randomizing the order in which items "a" through "g" appeared):

Q409. Which, if any, of the following do you believe in? Do you believe [INSERT] …

a. that Jesus rose from the dead, or not?

b. that God the father and Jesus Christ are separate, physical beings, or not?

c. that the president of (the LDS Church/the Mormon Church) is a prophet of God, or not?

d. that families can be bound together eternally in Temple ceremonies, or not?

e. that women who are dedicated members of (the LDS Church/the Mormon Church) should be ordained to the priesthood, or not?

f. in yoga, not just as exercise, but as a spiritual practice, or not?

g. in reincarnation, that people will be reborn in this world again and again, or not?[130]

Now, in the standard LDS context, a "belief" is something that can be defined as orthodox (or not) only by the Standard Works and the President of the Church. Although each Saint chooses to accept or not accept a belief personally, people who define themselves as 'believing Saints' typically base their religious beliefs on what they think the scriptures or the modern prophets have said.

As of the time this survey was conducted in 2011, the contents of the *Nauvoo Relief Society Minute Book* were either unavailable to the public, or had just barely become available. The vast majority of

---

[130] Pew Forum on Religion & Public Life (2012) p. 18. For a breakdown of results for each item, see Pew Research Center (2012) pp. 108-110.

3: Objections to Conferring Priesthood on LDS Women

Latter-day Saints—including most or all of the General Authorities of the Church, I would think—were completely unaware that Joseph Smith had said that "he was going to make of this [Relief] Society a kingdom of priests as in Enoch's day—as in Pauls day,"[131] or that "he spoke of delivering the keys to this [Relief] Society and to the church."[132] Under these circumstances, of course the typical believing Saint would conclude that the doctrine declared by the First Presidency did not include ordaining women to the Priesthood. Therefore, by a large margin, typical believing Saints would respond that he or she did not believe that LDS women should be ordained—*although a revelation announced by the Prophet of the Church would turn that completely around within a single day.*

The questionnaire used by the Pew Forum demonstrates no awareness of these issues in LDS culture: the LDS belief in continuing revelation; the role of the First Presidency in defining orthodox doctrine; the still-emergent nature of the teachings of Joseph Smith. In describing the extent to which the Pew researchers attempted to take LDS culture into consideration when designing their survey, all the report states is that "[t]he development of the survey questionnaire was informed by the advice and feedback received from a panel of advisers with expertise in the study of the U.S. Mormon population."[133] These advisers are nowhere identified in the report, but whoever they were, they did not seem to demonstrate much insider understanding of this aspect of LDS culture. That is most unfortunate.

It is a basic principle of survey research that "good questions [must be] ... valid (answers correspond to what they are intended to measure)."[134] Question #409(e) probably fails the validity test. If the researchers were trying to get at how Mormons feel about women's ordination, *given that the current Prophet of the Church has not opened*

---

[131] *Nauvoo Relief Society Minute Book* (1842-1844) p. 22.
[132] *Nauvoo Relief Society Minute Book* (1842-1844) p. 37.
[133] Pew Research Center (2012) pp. 70-71.
[134] Fowler (2002) p. 76.

the priesthood to women as of this moment in time, then I suppose the researchers do a 'good' job—although I must point out that this is a qualification that Pew could and should have made clear, if this was their objective. If the researchers were trying to get at how Mormons *would* feel about women's ordination, *if the Prophet of the Church approved it*, the researchers have utterly failed, and the item is definitely invalid. Certainly the breathless and thoughtless conclusions (*"Big majority of Mormons [including women] oppose women in priesthood"!*) drawn by so many people on the basis of this survey item are completely invalid.

What the Pew Forum questionnaire could and should have asked were any of the culturally sensitive questions mentioned by Alison Moore Smith in her clear analysis of the problems with the Pew survey:

- If offered the priesthood by the prophet, would you refuse it?
- If church leaders said women could be ordained would you support it?
- Would you welcome the ordination of women, if the general authorities approved it?
- Would you like it if women could righteously hold the priesthood?[135]

Without answers to questions like these, no one has the right to say anything about what Mormons in general, or LDS women in particular, feel about the ordination of women.

"Ordaining a woman would distract her attention from her husband and children."

I am surprised to hear the occasional informal statement made that if LDS women held the Priesthood, it would distract their atten-

---

[135] Alison Moore Smith (2014).

tion from the efforts they should be making on behalf of their husbands and children, and so therefore women should not have the priesthood. The logic here is exceedingly weak. This can be seen by simply applying the same logic to men. Could priesthood responsibilities possibly distract a man's attention from the efforts he should be making on behalf of his wife and children? If any readers are having trouble answering this question, I suggest that they speak with their ward's elders quorum president and bishop—and their wives and children. Case closed.

One of the challenges of being an adult male in the Church who is married and has children is balancing his roles as husband, father, Church member, priesthood holder, Church calling holder, provider/worker, and citizen. The distraction created by one's priesthood responsibilities against being a spouse and parent should be no greater for women than for men, and for most women, no greater than the distraction provided by being a diligent Relief Society member today.

"Well, men may have the priesthood, but women have motherhood!"

This has to be the downright silliest objection to women holding the priesthood that I have ever encountered. (A possible exception is the next one below—but it is a close call indeed).

Newsflash: the Earth has gone for long stretches, millennia at a time, without the Higher Priesthood being generally available. But motherhood has always been generally available to women, pretty much every single day of recorded secular history. One cannot bless so much as a single cup of water as part of the Sacrament of the Lord's Supper without a measure of the priesthood—but motherhood requires no such religious or spiritual prerequisites. By far, the vast majority (99.8%) of mothers in the world are not even Latter-day Saints. So in what ways is motherhood parallel to the priesthood? Exactly none.

"But then what would the poor *men* do?"

This falls within the domain of the You Can't Make This Stuff Up Department. Some people actually have said to me that ordaining women to the priesthood would create a terrible void in things for the brethren to do—because the more capable women would basically just take everything over.

As a man, I find this notion insulting in the extreme. I am second to none in my admiration for what women can do. However, the notion that 'the poor menfolk need protection from the overachieving women' is wrong on so many levels that it would require a separate book to address it appropriately—perhaps with a good stiff dose of psychoanalytic theory included, to boot.

Believe me, the brethren in the Church will have more than enough to do even if the sisters are ordained to the priesthood. Just think of the four-fold mission of the church:

1. **Proclaim the Gospel.** As of high noon on April 21, 2014, the U.S. Census Bureau estimated that there were about 7,161,083,901 people on the earth[136]; of these, only about 15,082,028 were Latter-day Saints[137] (a ratio of about 474 non-Latter-day Saints to 1 Saint, worldwide).

2. **Perfect the Saints.** The best rumors that I have heard place home teaching rates at 30% or less, perhaps much less, churchwide.

3. **Redeem the Dead.** The word on the street is that most temples outside of the Intermountain West are functioning nowhere near capacity.

4. **Care for the Poor and Needy.** The planet Earth is full to bursting at its seams with homeless, starving, diseased, and/or illiterate human beings, very often

---

[136] *U.S. and World Population Clock* (as of 12:00 noon EDT, April 21, 2014).
[137] "Statistical Report, 2013" (2014).

living in poverty. (Climate change will make all of this much worse, too.)

In short, there will still be an immense amount for men to do in a world where women also hold the priesthood. Let us put this notion to rest permanently. The manhood of LDS men would not be in any danger from women priesthood holders.

Summary

There is nothing at all in the Standard Works or revelation given to modern prophets that bars women from the priesthood. There is simply the repeated declaration that "this is God's way"—but saying this does not make it so, and repetition does not establish either matters of fact or divine truth.

4

The Real Reasons Why LDS Women Do Not Exercise the Priesthood in the Early 2010s

In Chapters 2 and 3, we saw that the reasons usually given for why the priesthood is not conferred upon LDS women are invalid. Before that, in Chapter 1, we saw that the Prophet Joseph Smith declared his intent to make the Relief Society into "a kingdom of priests," and that he said he was turning (perhaps some of) the keys of the kingdom to the leadership of the Relief Society. So why, then, do LDS women not exercise the priesthood today? In this chapter, I explain the real reasons why LDS women do not exercise the priesthood as of the early 2010s. There are essentially four reasons:

1. The tumult of the last two years of Joseph Smith's life, followed by his assassination, prevented him from following through on his teachings to the Relief Society.

2. The teaching of Emma Smith to the Relief Society against plural marriage alienated her from Church leadership. Emma's defection from the Saints nullified any priesthood keys that Joseph conveyed to the Relief Society presidency.

3. Brigham Young's negative experiences with Emma Smith made him mistrustful of her and the Relief Society, and disinclined to follow Joseph's lead regarding women and the priesthood.

4. The Saints as a whole, especially the leadership, were unaware of what Joseph Smith had taught to the Relief Society in 1842.

Below, I consider each of these reasons in turn.

1. Joseph Smith

One perceives in much of Joseph Smith's work as a prophet a pattern not unlike that of a spiral staircase: he would receive revelation regarding a Gospel concept, and then later in time he would revisit the issue and receive further revelation that brought that concept to a higher level of articulation and complexity. This process then might iterate again after some time, resulting in yet a deeper understanding of doctrine and practice. One might call this helical development, after the helix form made by a spiral staircase: as one ascends the stair, one repeatedly arrives at the same point on the circle, as it were—but at a higher level each time.

One can see this process at work in Joseph's understanding of temple ordinances. (Compare the endowment offered in Kirtland in 1836 and that offered in Nauvoo in 1842.) One sees this process at work in Joseph's developing understanding of priesthood offices. (The office of elder was introduced in Spring 1830, but the office of high priest in Spring 1831[138].) One sees this process at work even in Joseph's understanding of the name of the Church itself, which was first named "the Church of Christ" in 1830,[139] and then other names, with the name we know it by today, "The Church of Jesus Christ of Latter-day Saints," revealed to Joseph only in 1838.[140] Joseph's growth as an individual allowed him to receive more, and more complex, revelation, and this was reflected in the doctrine that he proclaimed, the social structures that he instituted, and the policies that he implemented for the Saints.

---

[138] "High Priest: Summary" (2014).
[139] D&C 20:1.
[140] D&C 115:4.

Joseph's assassination suddenly terminated his life and this process of helical development. It seems to have taken Joseph one to six years to revisit an issue as he ascended his helical staircase of doctrinal understanding. There simply was not enough time for Joseph to go further with his teachings about the Relief Society as "a kingdom of priest(esse)s," or with his actions with the Relief Society presidency and the keys of the kingdom, between the Spring of 1842 and June of 1844. Consider some of what was going on in Joseph's life during this period[141]:

- <u>**1841**</u>, April 6: Joseph lays the cornerstone for the Nauvoo Temple. Even though it is only half finished at the time of his assassination, its construction was a main concern for the Prophet for the next three years.
- <u>**1842**</u>, March: Joseph publishes the Book of Abraham.
- March 15: Joseph Smith becomes a Freemason. Thereafter he is involved in the growth of the Nauvoo Lodge, in which hundreds of LDS men were initiated in the space of just a couple of years.
- March 17: Joseph organizes the Relief Society.
- March 31: Joseph states, at the third meeting of the Relief Society, that "he was going to make of this Society a kingdom of priests."
- April 28: Joseph states that "I now turn the key to you" in the context of discussing the keys of the kingdom and the Relief Society leadership.
- May 4: Joseph Smith administers the ordinance of the LDS temple endowment for the first time, to himself and nine others. Thereafter, he is deeply in-

---

[141] Sources include Bushman (2005) and Hedges et al. (2011).

volved in conferring the blessings of the endowment ceremony upon a select group of Saints.

- May 19: Joseph is elected mayor of Nauvoo.
- May: Joseph is preoccupied with dealing with accusations against John C. Bennett, whom he disfellowshipped.
- July-November: Joseph is forced to deal with Bennett's regionally (then nationally) distributed anti-Mormon writings.
- August--October: Joseph goes into hiding to avoid being extradited to Missouri on a false charge of abetting the attempted murder of Missouri governor Lilburn W. Boggs.
- **1843**: Joseph and Emma are in repeated conflict around the issue of plural marriage.
- mid-June: Joseph learns that Missouri is pursuing extradition against him—again—for an old false charge of treason. He is arrested far from Nauvoo and is being transported under guard when a party of 100+ Saints from Nauvoo come to his rescue.
- August—December: Joseph deals with intense anti-Mormon sentiment, now promoted by the Whig party newspapers, and with kidnappings of Saints.
- September 28: Joseph and Emma become the first couple to receive the Second Anointing.
- **1844**, January 29: In a bid to bring the Saints' case to the public and the federal government, Joseph announces his candidacy for the American Presidency.
- February 20: With it being clear that Nauvoo could not endure against determined anti-Mormon armed

attacks, Joseph instructed the Twelve to send expeditions into the West to scout out places for the main body of the Saints to relocate.

- Spring: Joseph faces defections of several close associates to anti-Mormon groups.

- March: Joseph tells the Twelve that he had conferred all the keys upon them. He organizes the Council of Fifty privately, to govern the temporal kingdom of God. He meets with this Council weekly though the Spring to plan explorations in the West and to further his presidential campaign.

- April 7: Joseph preaches the King Follett discourse during General Conference.

- May: Joseph's enemies file charges against him in Carthage courts.

- June 27: After being arrested, and while he was in jail, Joseph is martyred with his brother Hyrum.

Essentially, in addition to all the added activity that came into Joseph's life with the revelation of the endowment ceremony, his American Presidential campaign, his mayoralty, Freemasonry, and so forth, Joseph had to contend with a great increase of intensity of external attack and internal dissension. This disrupted what would likely have been further development of the teachings he gave to the Relief Society in March and April of 1842.

Joseph's assassination, besides the pain it inflicted on his family, his associates, and the Church, also left many areas of doctrine and practice only partially resolved. These unresolved areas include such issues as the material he taught in the King Follett discourse—a cornucopia of new doctrine, although still not part of the Standard Works—and what he taught to the Relicf Society about the priesthood and women.

2. Emma Smith

Joseph's assassination was a seismic trauma for the Saints, on many levels. Among the many difficulties created by Joseph's death was an increasing degree of conflict between Joseph's widow, Emma Smith, and Brigham Young. Emma was president of the Relief Society. Brigham was President of the Quorum of the Twelve, and, within two months of the assassination, for all practical purposes, the acting President of the Church in all but name.

The two were in considerable conflict after Joseph's death.[142] Brigham thought that Emma's advice to Joseph Smith and Hyrum (both then in hiding in Iowa) to submit to the authorities—advice that led the Prophet and Patriarch right to Carthage jail, where they were assassinated—was catastrophically wrongheaded. Emma thought that Brigham and the Twelve were trying to cheat Emma and her children from property that was rightfully theirs. (Having Joseph's property intermingled with the Church's did not help matters any.) Brigham and Emma traded recriminations with each other even about the disposition of Joseph's clothing. During the succession crisis after Joseph's death, Emma had supported the claims of others over that of the Apostles and their leader, Brigham. Perhaps more than anything else, the two were split by the matter of plural marriage, which Brigham felt bound to support, and which Emma rejected with every fiber of her being to her very deathbed.

Emma began to preach against plural marriage in her capacity as president of the Relief Society at meetings in early 1844. As the authors of a history of Relief Society put it:

> The immediate difficulty [with the principle of plural marriage] was Emma's own, the climax to years of her struggle against the principle. But she enlisted her sisters in her battle, using the most powerful weapon she had: her position as president of the Re-

---

[142] Information in this paragraph is based on Arrington (1985/1986) pp. 117-119.

> lief Society.... [S]he opposed the practice her prophet-husband was promoting, thus bringing dissent into the inner circles of the Church. With each successive meeting that March [of 1844], she became more vehement in her demand for reformation .... In her strongest claim to validation, referencing the powers conferred on her in the organizational meeting two years earlier, she ended by claiming, as the minute taker wrote, "if their ever was any Authourity on the Earth she had it—and had it yet." Seeds of discord were sown, tares among the gospel's greening wheat.
>
> Emma's actions ... threatened the essential order and unity without which the Church could not survive.
>
> In pitting her authority against that of the prophet through whom her authority had come, and in planting disorder and disunity among the sisters, Emma Smith had erred egregiously.[143]

President John Taylor, then President of the Twelve, speaking at a general Relief Society meeting in Utah in 1880, said this of the situation in 1842-1844 Nauvoo:

> However after this organization [of the Relief Society] at Nauvoo, much disturbance arose among the sisters. I do not wish to be personal especially as Sister Emma is now dead, but I think that some of those circumstances should be known. Sister Emma got severely tried in her mind about the doctrine of Plural Marriage and she made use of the position she held to try to pervert the minds of the sisters in relation to that doctrine. She tried to influence my first wife and to make her believe that the revelation was not correct.... Soon after, the Prophet Joseph was in my

---

[143] Derr, Cannon, & Beecher (1992/2000) p. 62.

house and I spoke to him in my wife's presence, in relation to what sister Emma had said, and Joseph replied, "Sister Emma would dethrone Jehovah to accomplish her purpose if she could." ....

After the death of the Prophet Joseph, in consequence of the confusion then introduced President B. Young thought it best to defer the operations of this organization—and the labors of the Society ceased, until he organized the sisters again in this City [in 1867].

Those influences then introduced [in Nauvoo] and then operating were not right ....[144]

Emma—estranged from the new leadership of the Church, headed by Brigham Young, and ever opposed to plural marriage—would not accompany the Saints on the trek westward out of Nauvoo beginning in February 1846. Whatever keys of the kingdom had been turned to her by Joseph became of no consequence when Emma left the Church and cut herself off from priesthood authorities.

3. Brigham Young

In Brigham's eyes, one must imagine, Emma's lack of support for the Apostles' claim to Church leadership following Joseph's death was a threat to the Church itself, by draining support from those to whom Joseph had given the keys of the kingdom. Similarly, Emma's repeated and increasingly strident teaching against plural marriage, in Brigham's eyes, would not only have been a betrayal of Joseph's teachings, but a threat to the Church in a different way, by fueling internal dissent. All of this seems to have left Brigham with a marked distaste for women in positions of authority in the Church, a distaste that lasted for a generation.

In March 1845, Brigham told a meeting of the Seventy that women "have no right to meddle in the affairs of the Kingdom of

---

[144] "R.S. Reports" (1880) pp. 53-54.

God."[145] In this meeting, he stated, "When I want Sisters or the Wives of the members of the church to get up Relief Society I will summon them to my aid but until that time let them stay at home."[146] (He would not summon the Relief Society to his aid until 1867, when he had Eliza R. Snow—former plural wife of Joseph Smith, and then-current plural wife of Brigham himself—head a revived Relief Society.

4. Ignorance of Joseph's Teachings

In this book, we have considered some important and startling teachings given by Joseph Smith to the first Relief Society in March and April of 1842. As old as these teachings now are, they were not widely known at the time they were given, and they are still barely known in the Church as a whole.

So far as I have been able to discover, the contents of the *Nauvoo Relief Society Minute Book* have never been published by the Church, not in the 1840s, and not since. The important minutes were not excerpted in either the *Times and Seasons* or the *Nauvoo Neighbor*, for example. Some knowledge of the contents of the minutes remained with, say, Bathsheba W. Smith, the fourth Relief Society president, who physically possessed the *Minute Book* into the early years of the 20th century. However, following her death in 1910, the *Minute Book* passed into the Church Archives, where it was unavailable except to vetted researchers. It is only with the online release of documents

---

[145] Quoted in Quinn (1992) p. 373.
[146] Quoted in Derr, Cannon, & Beecher (1992/2000) p. 63. These authors note (p. 451 n. 18):
> The complete text [of Brigham's remarks to the Seventy] reveals an intensity of feeling unusual for Brigham Young and is indicative of the degree to which he considered the Church had been harmed by the women's actions.

That is, harmed by the Relief Society women's actions against plural marriage, taken under Emma Smith's leadership.

from the Joseph Smith Papers Project, beginning on June 5, 2012,[147] that the *Minute Book* has been available for all to inspect.

Although the four key passages of Joseph's teachings as mentioned in Table 1-1 (pp. 30-31 herein) are treated in a comprehensive history of Relief Society published by Deseret Book,[148] the numbers in Table 1-1 show quite starkly that three of these four passages have made absolutely no impact on official Church teaching or literature over at least the last 43 years, as of this writing.

Taken together, this evidence suggests that the leadership of the Church, from the days of Brigham Young to the present, simply have been unaware that Joseph Smith taught these things. One cannot implement teachings of which one is not aware.

One sometimes has the impression that at least someone in the leadership structure *is* aware of these teachings, but does not know what to do with them. Consider the current official history of the Relief Society, published by the Church directly, *Daughters of My Kingdom*.[149] This history quite laudably quotes or paraphrases text from the *Nauvoo Relief Society Minute Book* at least 38 times, by far the largest number of times that I have ever seen the *Minute Book* quoted in a single Church publication. This history specifically quotes Joseph Smith's teachings from the *Minute Book* 24 times. In 12 instances, this history quotes Joseph's teachings from the very pages of the *Minute Book* where one or the other of the "big four" of Joseph Smith's statements are made (see Table 1-1). However, only on a single occasion does this history actually quote one of the big four statements: "now I turn the key to you" [150] — without any hint that a few moments earlier, Joseph had been talking about delivering the keys of the kingdom.

In what seems to be a particularly egregious instance of selective quotation, *Daughters in My Kingdom* quotes in part one of the

---

[147] *2013 Church Almanac* (2012) p. 31, entry for June 5.
[148] Derr, Cannon, & Beecher (1992/2000) pp. 43-50, 53-54.
[149] *Daughters in My Kingdom* (2011).
[150] *Daughters in My Kingdom* (2011) pp. 14-15.

most telling passages of Joseph Smith's teachings to the Relief Society. In the *Minute Book*, this passage runs as follows:

> ... hence there should be a select Society separate from all the evils of the world, choice, virtuous and holy—**Said he was going to make of this Society a kingdom of priests as in Enoch's day—as in Pauls day** ....[151]

However, in the quotation given in *Daughters in My Kingdom*, the boldfaced portion of the quotation above is omitted.[152]

It would seem that it simply did not fit with the points that the authors of this manual were trying to make, anywhere in this history's 181 pages of main text, to mention that Joseph Smith "said he was going to make of this Society a kingdom of priests," that "he spoke of delivering the keys to this Society and to the church," that "the keys of the kingdom were about to be given to them [the sisters, i.e., the Relief Society leadership]." Or perhaps the authors simply did not know what to make of Joseph's teachings here. Either way, this is a terrible shame, and only contributes to the ignorance among Church members of these important teachings.

Summary

LDS women do not exercise the priesthood in the early 2010s because of a 'perfect storm' of circumstances dating to the period 1842-1846. Joseph Smith, who had taught the Relief Society important principles and had taken important actions regarding women and priesthood in the spring of 1842, was preoccupied with matters of personal and group survival from then until his death in 1844; these matters kept him from developing further what he had taught and the actions he had taken with the Relief Society in 1842.

---

[151] *Nauvoo Relief Society Minute Book* (1842-1844) p. 22, emphases added.
[152] *Daughters in My Kingdom* (2011) p. 15.

Joseph's wife Emma used her position as President of the Relief Society to take action against the practice of plural marriage; this, and her lack of support for the Twelve's leadership, estranged her further from the mainstream of the Church and its leadership, and once her estrangement was complete, Emma's journey out of the Church nullified whatever keys she possessed.

Brigham Young, faced with what was essentially the apostasy of Emma Smith, was disinclined to see women in leadership roles in the Church for more than a generation following Joseph's death. For that matter, Brigham may well not have known of Joseph's 1842 teachings to the Relief Society. Certainly there is no clear evidence that he did, nor that any of the current Church leadership is aware of these teachings either.

Of course, ignorance is a curable condition. When the leadership of the Church *does* become aware of these teachings, it is entirely possible that a change in priesthood practice may occur. What would that be like? I consider this in the following chapter.

5

The Future

In this chapter, I consider possible futures. Is it even possible that the practice of not conferring priesthood upon women in the Church might change? How might this occur? What might the body of the Saints do to resolve this issue—and what should they *not* do? Finally, what might a priesthood that included women look like?

Could change really happen?

For all practical purposes, the Restored Church has excluded women from the priesthood for over 180 years. Could change really occur now, at what seems to be a relatively late date?

Of course it could. This is the Restored Church, after all, where we believe in current revelation. One of our very Articles of Faith states that "we believe that He [God] will yet reveal many great and important things pertaining to the Kingdom of God."[153]

There once was a Church policy (often mistakenly called a 'doctrine') of exclusion men of African ancestry from the priesthood. The racial priesthood restriction had been started by Brigham Young in 1849. Over the years, it had been defended vehemently by many General Authorities of the Church and the First Presidency, as the unalterable word of God, as dating to the days of Joseph Smith, as rooted in the pre-mortal existence itself. In all of this the

---

[153] Pearl of Great Price, the Ninth Article of Faith.

authorities had been incorrect, but for complex historical reasons the Church continued to maintain this policy.[154]

On the afternoon of Friday, June 8, 1978, I casually dropped in to visit the Church building at Lincoln Center in Manhattan, New York City. (In that era, the building had a Visitors Center, and so was the sort of place that a fellow on a break from college and awaiting his mission call just might drop in.) A friend I met there told me that the racial priesthood restriction, which had been in effect for 129 years by that point, had just been dissolved by revelation to the Prophet. That very Sunday, my congregation, the Manhattan Second Ward, ordained its first black priesthood holder, Brother Titus Ifediba, later a member of the High Council of the New York New York Stake.

The Church turned around on a dime. It could happen again.

The reader should keep in mind that such a revelatory announcement, extending the priesthood to women, would in no way conflict with anything in the Standard Works, or revelation declared by modern prophets. (As we have seen in Chapters 2 and 3, there *are* no conflicting scriptures or modern revelations to cause concern.) In addition, such a revelation would be building upon what Joseph Smith himself taught to the Relief Society, as we saw in Chapter 1—teachings that were all but lost in the turmoil following Joseph's assassination, as described in Chapter 4.

How Might Such Change Occur?

Given that change is possible, how might it occur? As it happens, the history of the racial priesthood policy offers some clues.

Throughout the 1970s, the Church became increasingly aware that it was about to face a crisis of huge proportions because of its growth in places where the racial priesthood restriction created problems. From the late 1950s to the early 1960s, thousands of Nige-

---

[154] See: Bush (1969, 1973); Bush & Mauss (1984); Kimball (2005, p. 197 n. 3; 2008, p. 11 n. 6); Mauss (1967, 1981); "Race and the Priesthood" (2013).

rians had converted to the gospel through the study of Church pamphlet literature. Without anyone from the Church to baptize them, they had organized themselves into congregations, and requested the Church to send missionaries. In the early 1960s, however, the efforts of the Church to begin serious missionary work in Nigeria were thwarted by negative publicity in that country stemming from the Church's racial priesthood policy.[155]

By the mid-1970s, missionary work in Brazil had come face to face with a fascinating aspect of Brazilian demography. In Brazil, various races of people had intermarried freely for centuries, and enforcement of the priesthood ban would become quite problematic. President Spencer W. Kimball's decision in 1974 (the year he was set apart as President of the Church) to build a temple in Brazil only increased the internal pressure on the Church to deal in some fashion with the priesthood ban, which of course was also a temple ban.

Ultimately, the crises of the 1970 created a need to change the priesthood policy for the Church's future growth. Certainly this must have made the General Authorities of the time more receptive to hearing and supporting the revelation that President Kimball received, changing the priesthood policy.

As it happens, in our day, there exists a very different sort of internal crisis, or a collection of crises, that have relevance to the matter of restricting women from the priesthood. They are at least three in number: a crisis of pain; a crisis of testimony, and even defection; and, a crisis in sharing the Gospel. First, though, we must consider the basis for the crises.

Basis for the Crises

Human society has changed from the time the Relief Society was organized in 1842. As LDS author and prominent business figure Sheri Dew has described that era:

---

[155] Prince & Wright (2005) pp. 81-87, 90-91; see also pp. 92-94.

> ... [S]ociety at large was still highly patriarchal and, as such, strictly limiting of women's rights. Women couldn't vote, let alone hold office or even exert political influence. (The landmark Seneca Falls Convention, where the push for women's suffrage began in earnest, was still six years away.) Most women were denied higher education, and many weren't formally educated at all. Few had any way of earning money, and if a woman did earn a wage, it legally belonged to her husband. It was still unusual for women to own property. And some physical violence against women was not only tolerated socially but protected by law! The bottom line? In 1842, many still viewed women as being just a rung higher on the social ladder than prisoners.[156]

The national situation was not substantially improved by the time Brigham Young revived the Relief Society in 1867. Sometimes the general society's resistance to women's desire to increase their knowledge and express their talents was expressed in ways both personal and vulgar.

> In 1869, a few women who had wrangled their way into the clinical lectures at Pennsylvania Hospital entered the amphitheater to hisses, yowls, mock applause, and "offensive remarks upon personal appearance." During the final hour of the lecture, a Philadelphia paper reported, "missiles of tinfoil ... were thrown upon the ladies while some of the men defiled the dresses of the ladies near them with tobacco juice."[157]

The women of the United States did not all receive the right to vote until 1920 (and then, only after years of legislative battles and

---

[156] Dew (2013) Kindle locations 1769-1774.
[157] Collins (2003/2007) pp. 242-243.

5: The Future

demonstrations in which "suffragists were shot at and dragged down the street by people attempting to wrest away their banners"[158]). In today's era of increased longevity, 1920 is still within living memory.[159] Discrimination against women has continued for decades since 1920.

> In the period 1925-1945 American medical schools placed a 5 percent quota on female admissions. In the 1920s Columbia and Harvard law schools still excluded women applicants, and until 1937 so did the New York City Bar Association.[160]
>
> [After the passage of the Civil Rights Act in 1964:] The newly created Equal Employment Opportunity Commission .... made its disinterest in the woman's issue evident in 1965, when it ruled that newspaper help-wanted ads could no longer discriminate on the basis of race, religion, or national origin, but that it was okay to continue dividing them into "Male Help Wanted" and "Female Help Wanted" sections.[161]
>
> At the beginning of the 1970s ... the *New York Times* printed a story about a woman attempting to rent an apartment who was forced to get her husband, a mental hospital patient, to cosign the lease. A wealthy middle-aged divorcée who wanted to buy a co-op had to get her father's signature on the contract. Mortgage lenders frequently refused to count a wife's salary in determining family income under the

---

[158] Collins (2003/2007) p. 312.

[159] Speaking of the fact that all women in the U.S. did not receive the right to vote until 1920, the entertainer Louis CK recently noted, "That means American democracy is 94 years old. There are three people in my building older than American democracy" ("Louis CK monologue," 2014, time marker 7:55-8:06 min.).

[160] Hymowitz & Weissman (1978) p. 307.

[161] Collins (2003/2007) p. 435.

> theory that she would stop working and have babies—although some offered to make exceptions for anyone who could prove she'd had a hysterectomy. Divorced women were regarded as high risks by insurance companies, and they had trouble getting credit cards....
>
> ... In North Carolina, only a virgin could charge a man with rape. In Alabama, the idea of women serving on juries was still something of a novelty—the courts had only ordered the state to include them in 1966.[162]

It was only in the 1970s that

> Congress banned discrimination in credit, and required schools that got public money to treat boys and girls equally. Medical schools and law schools, which often set a flat 5 percent cap on female students, were forced to open their doors. The number of women medical school graduates rose from 7.5 percent in 1969 to nearly 20 percent in 1976.[163]

Despite the Equal Pay Act of 1963, significant pay disparity by gender remains an issue today. Beyond that, "we have a culture that still places a different set of expectations and burdens on women and that still nudges or even shames them into certain roles."[164]

However, change has come, especially to the societies of the West, and especially since 1970. In the early 2010s, more than half of undergraduate and graduate degrees are earned by women. With education can come an awakening of the sense of one's powers and capabilities. So it is that we have come to see some American women head major military organizations, corporations, and universi-

---

[162] Collins (2003/2007) p. 438.
[163] Collins (2003/2007) p. 446.
[164] Bruni (2014) p. 3.

ties. In postwar Europe, we have seen women as the prime ministers of Great Britain and Germany. At this writing in April of 2014, the names of several women are being proposed in national forums as credible candidates for the American presidency in advance of the 2016 election.

The reason for this trip through recent history is to show how radically the world has changed for American women over just the last 40 years or so. Women's educational and career opportunities have expanded tremendously over this period—and, with those expansions, there has come a corresponding broadening of women's ideas about what they can do with their lives.

In the Church, where education is particularly encouraged, women as a group are even better educated than women in some other religious groups. Here, too, it is only to be expected that women will wish to be the most that they can be in many spheres.

In 21st century industrialized societies throughout the world, women are coming to discover that they can do this, and hold the same responsibilities, and have the same opportunities, as men. The sole exception to that is within the priesthood or its equivalent within certain religious groups, of which the Church is a notable example.

We have now reached a point where that situation is becoming less tolerable for the membership of the Church. Let us now consider those three crises.

A Crisis of Pain

Neylan McBaine put it this way in her presentation at the 2012 conference of the Foundation for Apologetic Information and Research (FAIR), describing her research on women in the Church:

> I came to rest on a prominent, consistent theme: There is a tremendous amount of pain among our women regarding how they can or cannot contribute to the governance of our ecclesiastical organization, and we need to pay attention to that pain. Listen to

these statements, recently gathered across a variety of forums: "My 12-year-old son gets the priesthood and all of a sudden he's got more power and authority than me!" Or another: "I truly wish you could feel the pain I feel as a woman in the Church. I know my potential and worth, and to have it limited to the role of 'presidee' in all areas discredits me as a daughter of God." Or this one: "I feel like if I had been a 'good' Mormon, I wouldn't have gotten my Master's degree. I wouldn't be working now, and I wouldn't WANT to work so much. I'd want to be a mother and have kids and stay home." Lastly: "I have a PhD and am a full-time professor at a university. I am also married and have three children. The only place in my life where I am treated like a lesser human being is at church." I could go on and on.[165]

This is the first crisis, the crisis of pain. Whatever the situation may have been in late 1997, when President Hinckley spoke with Australian television, it is certainly not the case almost a generation later—certainly not universally—that "our [LDS] women are happy" and "satisfied"[166] with the way things are regarding the priesthood. Reading the comments of women in the Mormon blogosphere puts the lie to the idea that women who are in pain over this issue have shaky testimonies or are looking to justify personal apostasy; such pre-judgments are naïve and condescending.

But there are yet two crises to go. For a substantial number of Saints, it does not take long for personal pain and misgivings to become evident in crises of faith and even defection.

---

[165] McBaine (2012) pp. 71-72.
[166] "Compass interview" (1997).

A Crisis of Testimony—and Defection

A study published in 2012 by the Mormon Research Foundation (a small private organization) paints a disturbing picture of the corrosive effect upon testimony that personal doubts about the Church's policies on women and the priesthood have had, for thousands of Church members. The study was conducted online in 2011, and surveyed "people who once believed that the Church is 'the only true and living church upon the face of the whole earth' (D&C 1:30), but who no longer believe that it is."[167] Of the 3086 people in the sample, 58% were male and 42% female; the typical respondent was a married (70%) college graduate (39%) living in the United States but outside of Utah (60%), earning $80K-$200K annually (36%). Many had served full-time missions for the Church (73% of the men, 17% of the women), and had served in various leadership positions in the Church (over 50% of the men, 40% of the women). Twenty percent of the sample still attended Church weekly, while 56% did not attend Church meetings any more at the time the survey was administered.[168]

When asked to rank a list of 41 possible issues that may have had an impact on their losing belief in the Church, the typical participant (46%) noted more than 15 issues as being either "a major factor" or "the primary factor." "[T]here was not simply one or two issues that led to disbelief; on the contrary, many issues appeared to 'stack up' until belief was lost."[169] However, the matter of women's issues in the Church were prominent among the issues mentioned for losing faith in the Church. Major findings in this regard include the following:

- Of the whole sample, 47% stated that the "Church's stance on women" was either a major factor or the

---

[167] Mormon Research Foundation (2012) p. 4.
[168] Mormon Research Foundation (2012) pp. 4-6.
[169] Mormon Research Foundation (2012) p. 8. See also "Why do you no longer believe" (n.d.).

primary factor in their loss of faith in the Church.[170] The results also show that, over time, this issue is *increasing* in importance in the loss of faith.[171]

- In terms of historical issues that negatively affected their belief, 40% of the whole sample stated that "Women and the Priesthood" was either a major factor or the primary factor in their loss of faith in the Church.[172]

Respondents had the opportunity to make comments as well as answer questions on the survey. The researchers noted this about some of the comments:

> Further analysis of the open comments submitted by **female respondents** showed some common themes:
>
> - *Men presiding over/making decisions for women.* Examples: "I also could no longer support an organization that believes men have the divine right to preside over women." "I truly wish you could feel the pain I feel as a woman in the church. I know my potential and worth, and to have it limited to the role of "presidee" in all areas discredits me as a daughter of God."
>
> - *General inequality towards women.* Examples: …. "At church I was not valued for my talents or contributions in the same way, nor treated equally as men (a 12 year old boy had more authority from God than I did)."
>
> - *Women and the Priesthood.* Examples: "Give women the priesthood." "Why am I reading ac-

---

[170] Mormon Research Foundation (2012) p. 8.
[171] Mormon Research Foundation (2012) p. 10.
[172] Mormon Research Foundation (2012) p. 9.

> counts of Joseph Smith giving the Priesthood to Women. What happened? What is the real story, and when are we going to start teaching it?"[173]

There is much that could be said about these findings, and the freeform comments quoted above. Perhaps the most important thing to point out for the topic at hand is that, based on these findings, it looks like the matter of LDS women and the priesthood is a weighty factor in the loss of faith that many Saints have experienced. Even beyond this, it appears that the number of Saints experiencing this loss of faith is growing.

Early in 2012, the Reuters news agency interviewed Elder Marlin Jensen, then a member of the Presidency of the Seventy, regarding attrition in the Church. The news was not good.

> Jensen, the church's official historian, would not provide any figures on the rate of defections, but he told Reuters that attrition has accelerated in the last five or 10 years, reflecting greater secularization of society. ….
>
> Not since a famous troublespot in Mormon history, the 1837 failure of a church bank in Kirtland, Ohio, have so many left the church, Jensen said. "Maybe since Kirtland, we've never had a period of—I'll call it apostasy, like we're having now," he told [a] group in Logan.[174]

So this is the crisis of testimony and defection that the Church faces today. If the Mormon Research Foundation's survey findings apply here, then the matter of LDS women and the priesthood is playing a substantial role in these defections from the Church.

---

[173] Mormon Research Foundation (2012) p. 13.
[174] Henderson & Cooke (2012).

A Crisis in Sharing the Gospel

Finally, the current situation with LDS women and the priesthood has, I suspect, a highly negative impact on spreading the gospel in many populations, especially in the industrialized West.

As a younger man, I attended Haverford College in the Main Line suburbs of Philadelphia. At the time, Haverford was a men's college. (It since has become fully coeducational.) For three years, I took part in the official dormitory exchange at nearby Bryn Mawr College, then and now a women's college. My college experience involved intense discussions on all variety of subjects, largely with some of the brightest college women in North America. In our discussions, the matter of my Mormonism would come up. The women (as well as some Haverford men) asking the questions about my religion often had complimentary things to say. However—especially at Bryn Mawr—the matter of women's not being eligible to receive the LDS priesthood inevitably arose, and I felt doors shut, repeatedly. When I was asked why it was that LDS women were not so ordained, all I could say was some variety or other of "only God knows." This was not considered to be a particularly strong response.

So it was that some of the very brightest lights among college women felt confirmed in their desire to terminate further discussion of my LDS faith, because in their eyes, it simply recapitulated the sexist actions of other religions. Very rarely did we get to a place where they would accept a copy of the Book of Mormon from me and pray to know whether it was true—because, in their eyes, any religion that did not ordain women to their clergy, by that very fact, simply could not be true to start with.

It is now many years later. I currently live in midtown Manhattan in New York City. I walk daily among the skyscrapers of Midtown, buildings occupied by the offices of people who are largely graduates of the most prominent colleges and universities in the nation. In the course of my work as a research entrepreneur or as a writer, it is not unusual for me to meet with these people, for business or socially. Frequently enough—typically because my abstention from coffee, alcohol, and so forth is noticeable—the subject of my LDS faith comes up. Often enough, I feel those same doors closing, both for the women and for the men. (For what man wants to explain to his highly educated female significant other that he is investigating a religion that does not ordain women?)

My sense of the situation is that this story is repeated in all the major cities of America and Europe. Educated people look at the LDS practice regarding women and the priesthood, and they rule the Church out of consideration. It is not even necessarily the practice that is the problem: it is the unavailability of any substantial support for the current LDS practice, beyond a reiteration of "well, it's the Lord's way"—something that rings hollow to many outside the Church, and to many inside as well.

I have no statistics to share on this matter. The Church does not report the number of people who were *not* baptized as converts, let alone why (and of course does not even collect this information to the best of my knowledge). Perhaps the Church's research arm has commissioned focus groups to explore the reasons people do *not* engage the Church, but if so, they have not made those findings public. However, I do have the experience of over half my life living in a City that is a microcosm of the Western world, and that experience tells me that the current LDS practice—barring women from the priesthood without any solid explanation—has been hurting the Church's mission of sharing the gospel, at least in the industrialized West, for some time. In a world where more and more women are receiving higher education every year, this crisis is not going to go away, and can only get worse.

We have our crises surrounding the issue of women in the priesthood. Across the history of the Church, in times of crisis, it has not been uncommon for the President of the Church to seek guidance from the Lord, often after an extended period of much prayer on the matter. Often enough, the Lord responds, sometimes quite forcefully. And when that happens, on this issue, we may see change.

Am I saying that the Prophet must have a revelation for change to occur in the matter of LDS women and the priesthood? Of course I am. It has been over 170 years since Joseph Smith made the last of his pivotal discourses on women and the priesthood to the Nauvoo Relief Society. Great numbers of Saints have been under the mistaken impression that the restriction barring women from the priesthood is doctrinally based. A similar situation faced the Church in 1978 with the racial priesthood restriction; it had been over 100 years since the Saints had ordained Black men, and great numbers of Saints had been under the mistaken impression that the racial priesthood restriction was doctrinally based. A revelation was needed in 1978, and a revelation will be needed now.

What the Saints Might Do—and Not Do

It would not surprise me in the slightest if one or more readers of this book came away with the notion that the thing to do is to have the Church extend the priesthood to women. Then, being Latter-day Saints (as I imagine most of my readers to be), the next step inevitably must be action.

The Latter-day Saints are a people focused on action, behavior, doing. Our history has shaped us this way; the trials of persecution, followed by the challenges involved in trying to create a civilization in a hostile environment in the Intermountain West, created a body of Saints focused on getting things done. It thus would be natural for a Saint reading this book to wonder, what can I do to further this process, and obtain some resolution of the issue of LDS women and the priesthood? I have some suggestions, both positive and negative.

Negative Suggestion:
Do *not* try to force the Lord's or the Prophet's hands.

I am sorry to have to start off my list of suggestions with a "don't." However, recent events force me to make this suggestion a top priority. In late March and early April 2014, there was a series of interchanges between the Church and a movement of women that wished to attend the Priesthood Session of April 2014 General Conference. Other such interchanges have occurred before, and likely will again. I consider this very unfortunate and counterproductive.

All of this has happened before. The decade of the 1960s saw a great deal of publicity focused on the Church's racial priesthood restriction, in the context of the American national debate regarding civil rights for people of all races. The Church was publicly criticized by the Utah branch of the National Association for the Advancement of Colored People (NAACP) because of the Church's priesthood policy; Nigeria refused to issue visas to LDS missionaries for the same reason; a campaign was held to encourage universities to severe athletic ties with Brigham Young University.[175]

No doubt many of those who protested the Church's racial priesthood restriction thought that by doing so they would be encouraging the Church to change that practice. However, all evidence suggests that exactly the opposite was the case: protests hardened leaders' resolve against changing the racial priesthood restriction, precisely to underscore the point that the Church is run by revelation, rather than by public opinion. The biographers of President David O. McKay made this point in describing his reaction to NAACP complaints about the Church's practice in 1963:

> McKay was not a man to be pushed and ... had reacted strongly to pressure from the outside by saying, "We shall make no concession to the NAACP.

---

[175] Kimball (2005) p. 202; Mauss (1981) pp. 14-16, 18.

> They are trying to take advantage of the situation to make the Church yield equality in the Church."[176]

The demonstrations by the NAACP and others did not further the repeal of the racial priesthood restriction. If anything, my sense of the situation is that they *delayed* that repeal, in order to avoid the impression that the Church or its President were being 'made to yield,' in President McKay's phrase. And I say this, believing that that delay may have been dictated by the Lord.

The desire to avoid the appearance of giving in to outside pressure—a desire that may be divine in origin, in this case—was important in the history of the racial priesthood restriction. In the Spring of 1978, I conducted an independent study research project as an undergraduate at Haverford College, under the mentorship of the late Richard Luman, then chair of the Religion Department. I undertook to survey everything that had been published in the major outlets of the national press (*The New York Times*, the *American Mercury*, etc.) from 1900 to early 1978, and to chart how the attention given to different topics changed over the years. Among my little discoveries was the fact that the attention paid by the print media to the matter of the racial priesthood restriction had declined radically after 1970, to an all-time low by the spring of 1978. This nugget sprang to mind less than two months after my project was completed, when the racial priesthood restriction was repealed.

Directly confrontational actions (demonstrations, non-negotiable demands) are not just divisive, they are counterproductive. One cannot storm Temple Square like the Bastille (literally or figuratively) and expect to force the Lord's or the Prophet's hands on the issue.

So don't demonstrate on Temple Square. Don't flood the General Authorities' mailboxes with copies of this book. (I am quite confident that this book will find its proper readers without such an irritation.) Don't send petitions to the First Presidency. And I pray that no one does anything so utterly pointless as to actually ordain a

---

[176] Prince & Wright (2005) p. 88.

woman on their own initiative. (This was done on a couple of occasions with Black men, before President Kimball received the revelation reversing the racial priesthood restriction. It merely resulted in the excommunications of all parties involved.)

Come now! We are Latter-day Saints! We either believe this religion, or we don't. If one doesn't believe it at all, this is all a moot point. But if one believes that the President of the Church is truly a Prophet, holding the keys to the priesthood, then it is self-contradictory to attempt to perform priesthood ordinances that the Prophet has not authorized. We can all act more like smart Saints here.

I am not counseling inaction. Below, I counsel a different kind of action.

There are two principles I have had impressed upon me as I have written this book, in terms of how to facilitate a positive resolution of the issue of LDS women and the priesthood. The first is a statement attributed to R. Buckminster Fuller:

> You never change things by fighting the existing reality. To change something, build a new model that makes the existing model obsolete.

The second principle is an ancient one. My guess is that some of my own ancestors were among those who studied the Jewish mystical discipline, the Kabbalah, at the time that the multivolume text known as the *Zohar* emerged in Spain, seven centuries ago. If my guess is correct, then these ancestors would have learned this principle: "the upper world moves in response to the lower world."[177] What we do Here makes a difference There—which in response may well create a development Here that we could not have accomplished on our own. In the spirit of these principles, I offer several positive suggestions.

---

[177] *Zohar* 164a; see Sperling & Simon (1984) p. 129.

Positive Suggestion #1:
Prayer

No doubt some readers will consider the suggestion of prayer to be a cop-out. I would hope that no Latter-day Saints would think this. I have witnessed outright miracles come as a result of prayer, as have many of the Saints. So, brothers and sisters both: let us pray. And pray for what?

- Pray that the Lord will send His word to His Prophet regarding the matter of LDS women and the priesthood.

- Pray that the presiding brethren remember the Lord's word to every high council in the Church—including the highest high council:

    > In case of difficulty respecting doctrine or principle, if there is not a sufficiency written to make the case clear to the midst of the council, the president may inquire and obtain the mind of the Lord by revelation.[178]

    There certainly "is not a sufficiency written" in the scriptures or modern revelation to restrict women from the priesthood. There is *nothing* written to support that idea.

- Pray that every LDS women will find her way to express her talents and potentials, and take the best advantage of her opportunities, while continuing as a vital part of the Gospel community.

- Pray that every LDS man will treat women as the goddesses-in-embryo that they are—and vice versa.

---

[178] D&C 102:23.

- Pray that the Church comes to grips in a productive way with the teachings of Joseph Smith to the Nauvoo Relief Society in the Spring of 1842.

**Positive Suggestion #2:
Frame the priesthood issue differently.**

In my research for this book, I was heartbroken to read accounts like the following (former BYU professor Valerie Hudson's experience):

> In the spring of 1996, I was driving my then-nine-year-old daughter, Ariel, to judo class. She was unusually quiet and I knew why. For years, when anyone had asked her what she wanted to be when she grew up, she would answer, "President of the United States, prophet of the Church, a mother, a botanist, a teacher and a ballet dancer." This had been the topic of conversation just before we got in the car and her older brother had cavalierly informed her that there was no way she could be prophet of the Church—that only men could be the prophet. We drove along in silence for several blocks and then she turned to me, her chin quivering, and asked, "Mom, is it true? Is it true women can't be prophet?" I told her it was true. She began to cry in earnest. I realized this was a major turning point in my daughter's life. For the very first time, she saw that her gender constrained who she could be. My heart broke for her, broke for the loss of something she might never regain—the feeling that who Ariel was was more important than the fact that she was a girl.[179]

Allow me to suggest a different way to frame the issue than the way that Ariel's brother did. As I noted in Chapter 3, Elder John

---

[179] Quoted in McBaine (2012) p. 77.

Taylor taught an assembly of Saints in 1857 that "you have been ordained kings and queens, and priests and priestesses to your Lord."[180] This was taught in public in the Bowery in Salt Lake City, and published by Bookcraft in *The Gospel Kingdom*, G. Homer Durham's collection of John Taylor's sermons, in 1941 and again in 1987. No secret, this.

Certainly Elder Taylor's remarks establish, at the very, very least, that women shall be priestesses to the Lord at some point. We can tell that to our children and grandchildren—both the girls *and* the boys—and when the inevitable question comes up on the question of when, we can say that this is a very good question, and perhaps we should all pray to the Lord to reveal that answer.

Don't focus on what a young girl can't do now. There are lots of things that a young girl can't do now, including vote *or* run for President of the United States. These are each activities that she can do at defined times in the future. Ordination to the priesthood is not on such a defined timeline—but it will come, according to Elder Taylor. Focus on what all women will be able to do—someday.

Is this perfect? Of course not. But it is the truth, and it puts the emphasis on futures and possibilities—something appropriate for all LDS adults to do.

Positive Suggestion #3:
Integrate women more fully into the local councils of the Church.

Neylan McBaine makes excellent suggestions that local Church leaders can implement immediately to integrate women more into the local councils of the Church.[181] Her suggestions are detailed and easily available online, so I shall not repeat them here. Suffice it to say that her suggestions are appropriate to both women and men,

---

[180] Taylor (1858), also quoted in Taylor (1941/1987) pp. 221-222.
[181] McBaine (2012), especially "Part V: The Internal Shift."

including ward and stake leadership, and many of them can be implemented immediately.

Positive Suggestion #4:
Familiarize the Church with the teachings of Joseph Smith to the Nauvoo Relief Society

As of this writing, the *Nauvoo Relief Society Minute Book* is online at the Joseph Smith Papers Project website. (See the References list for the URL. Readers may find it most convenient to consult the clear typescript on the website, rather than the handwritten pages, but to each their own.)

I would suggest that we all familiarize ourselves with the more crucial passages of the *Minute Book* at the very least, including Joseph Smith's remarks at the third and sixth meetings of the Relief Society. Let us use these teachings of Joseph Smith in *our* teaching in Church classes, and in our preaching in Sacrament Meeting, as appropriate.

Positive Suggestion #5:
Ask people to source their doctrinal claims.

This suggestion is very simple. When confronted with a Latter-day Saint making doctrinal or policy claims that sound 'off,' if the Spirit dictates, simply ask: "Where does it say that?" We may occasionally need to follow that up with the question "But is that declared as a revelation by the President of the Church?" As the Saints at the local level come to understand the need to ground our claims about doctrine or policy on a solid foundation, we may reasonably hope that this notion "trickles up," as it were.

What a Priesthood with Women Might Look Like

So let us say it happens. Conditions seem favorable. We certainly have our current internal crises, parallel to the internal crises that existed before the repeal of the racial priesthood restriction. We certainly have the record of Elder John Taylor's teachings regarding Latter-day Saint priestesses, very roughly parallel to the statements made by LDS prophets in the 19th and 20th centuries that in the future Black men would receive the priesthood. Most especially, we now have the teachings of Joseph Smith to the Nauvoo Relief Society in the spring of 1842, with their powerful implications for the matter of women and the priesthood.

It may well be the case that someday in the future—perhaps the very near future—the Prophet and President of the Church will seek revelation from the Lord to clarify the situation of women and the priesthood. Just hypothetically, let us say that the Lord reveals that women are to receive the priesthood immediately.

Then what? What would that look like?

There are several different scenarios for what a priesthood with worthy women might look like, including (but certainly not limited to) the following:

- Women have the Melchizedek Priesthood conferred upon them, and are ordained to the same offices that currently exist. Women may continue to be organized in gender-specific groups or quorums.

- Women have the Melchizedek Priesthood conferred upon them, and are ordained to different, women-only offices.

- Women have a different order of priesthood conferred upon them (perhaps named after a different scriptural figure altogether) which may have similar or entirely different offices compared to those of the Melchizedek Priesthood.

What is important to note here is that *all priesthood offices are merely appendages to the Priesthood itself*, a principle that was revealed to the Prophet Joseph in 1832,[182] and again in 1835.[183] We must not

---

[182] D&C 84:29.

forget that the true name of the Priesthood is "the Holy Priesthood, after the Order of the Son of God."[184] Everything else, all offices and orders, are an appendage, subordinate to the Priesthood itself. Whether it be the same offices for women as for men or different offices is immaterial. The Lord will work out the details, if we let Him and are receptive to Him.

And receptivity to what the Lord has to say, even against our own preconceptions, is key. Joseph Smith deserves the last word here: [185]

> Who knows the mind of God? Does he not reveal things differently from what we expect?

---

[183] D&C 107:5.
[184] D&C 107:3.
[185] *Nauvoo Relief Society Minute Book* (1842-1844) pp. 37-38.

6

Further Objections

In this chapter, I address more general objections to my case—and to me as the author of it.

"The book is already closed on this subject."

Some readers might object, "The Church has just published something about this on the Church website.[186] Doesn't such an authoritative statement close the book on the issue, so to speak?"

Not at all. Although the Church website is an outlet for official Church announcements and news releases, and for learning aids such as the topic pages, these web pages are in no way "authoritative" for defining Church doctrine.

"If the Brethren have not changed this already, surely there is a reason."

Some readers might object, "If your case were true, then why wouldn't the Brethren already have taken care of this and conferred the priesthood on LDS women? The fact that the Brethren have *not* done this itself proves that there is some kind of impediment to women's ordination."

No. Not really.

Here again, the history of the racial priesthood restriction is useful. For at least a century, from Brigham's declaration in 1849 through the First Presidency's official statement in 1949, the Breth-

---

[186] "Women in the Church."

ren proclaimed in sermons, conference addresses, and First Presidency official statements that Black men could not hold the priesthood, as a matter of doctrine, justifying their position with a number of scriptural interpretations and references to the pre-mortal existence.

Then, beginning with President David O. McKay, this entire superstructure of "doctrine" and practice began to crumble. Following his 1954 trip to the South Africa Mission, President McKay stated in a private conversation that

> There is not now, and there never has been a doctrine in this Church that the Negroes are under a divine curse. ... *It is a practice, not a doctrine, and the practice will some day be changed.*[187]

President McKay took another step. As related by the later Church Historian, Leonard J. Arrington:

> A special committee of the Twelve appointed by President McKay in 1954 to study the issue concluded that there was no sound scriptural basis for the policy but that the church membership was not prepared for its reversal.[188]

That is quite interesting. For a century, the Brethren had declared a position to be doctrinally based (although the supposed "doctrine" was based on shaky interpretations of scripture, and a formal revelation of God had never been received on the matter).

Then, with the world having changed by the mid-1950s, the President of the Church commissions a group of Brethren to study the matter out, and they conclude that there is no basis at all for the policy—but *the attitudes of the Church membership itself stood in the way of change.*

---

[187] Quoted in Prince & Wright (2005) pp. 79-80, emphasis in original. Pres. McKay, years later, confirmed this account of his remarks (Prince & Wright, 2005, p. 97).

[188] Quoted in Prince & Wright (2005) p. 80.

The priesthood would not be extended to Black men for another 24 years after President McKay's commission concluded that there was "no sound scriptural basis for the policy." Now, of course, the Church categorically rejects each and all of the arguments that its leaders had once advanced to support the racial priesthood restriction.[189]

Does any of this sound at all applicable to the matter of LDS women and the priesthood?

So, no, I do not accept the logic that says, since the Brethren have not extended the priesthood to women, this means there must be some solid doctrinal reason for this. If there is a reason at all, I think it is best described in the same words used by President McKay's commission in 1954: there is no sound scriptural basis for the policy, but the church membership—or some part thereof—has not heretofore been prepared for its reversal.

"You're making mountains of molehills."

I can imagine readers saying that I have made a great deal out of a few pages in the *Nauvoo Relief Society Minute Book*. Fair enough. But I would enjoin such readers to consider other occasions where a brief record has had momentous implications.

The entire account of Joseph Smith's First Vision as we have it in the Pearl of Great Price comprises one single sheet of printed paper, in the 1981 edition of the scriptures. (It only extends onto nine lines of one column of the second side of that sheet of paper.) And yet the personal spiritual testimony of the truth of what is printed on that single sheet of paper has brought into the Church millions of converts—including myself.

The Joseph Smith's King Follett discourse, as most Church readers are familiar with it, is 21 pages long.[190] What I would con-

---

[189] "Race and the Priesthood" (2013).
[190] J. F. Smith (1938) pp. 342-362.

sider the heart of this discourse is only 10 pages long.[191] Yet this portion—containing, as it does, clear teaching about the nature of God as an exalted Man, the eternity of matter and intelligence, and much more—contains an utterly groundbreaking understanding of the nature of humanity, divinity, the physical universe, and the relationship among them. Its vision that every human being is divine nobility capable of attaining godhood, and that God and Human are essentially the same species of being, has inspired me, and changed my life, since I first read it almost four decades ago. There is a reason why one of the foremost cultural critics of the 20th century, Harold Bloom, called the King Follett discourse "certainly one of the truly remarkable sermons ever preached in America."[192]

Finally, consider what we now know as Official Declaration—2, which extends the priesthood to all worthy males regardless of race. OD—2 takes up about one and a half pages in the Doctrine and Covenants, although the heart of the matter, the letter of the First Presidency dated June 8, 1978, takes but a single page. And yet the occasion of the reception of the revelation behind this letter was, according to President Spencer W. Kimball, "the most earthshaking thing that has happened in my lifetime."[193]

Yes, I am largely building my case here on a few key statements made by Joseph Smith in the *Nauvoo Relief Society Minute Book*. But as the examples above show, the sheer volume of a statement is no measure of its importance or its potential impact. I am also reminded that, in the book of Genesis, the Lord is recorded as beginning the creation of the world with only two words: יְהִי אוֹר *Y'hi Or*, translated as "Let there be light!"[194]

---

[191] From the beginning of the section headed "God an Exalted Man" through the end of the section headed "The Relation of Man to God" (pp. 345-355).

[192] Bloom (1992) p. 95.

[193] Kimball (2005) p. 231.

[194] Genesis 1:3 (capitalization and exclamation point added).

"You are going to shake a lot of people's testimonies and faith in the General Authorities with what you've written."

There may be some readers who feel that my presentation, in which I mention several times that not everything said by a General Authority is necessarily the word of God, will hurt people's testimonies and faith in the General Authorities. There are several things to be pointed out here.

First and foremost, we're not supposed to base our faith on the General Authorities. *That* is the sort of thing that is a weak basis for a testimony. In Chapter 2, I quote Joseph Smith, Harold B. Lee, Joseph Fielding Smith, and Dieter F. Uchtdorf, teaching principles like the fallibility of the General Authorities, and how the Standard Works and revelation to the Prophet must be our guide.[195]

Secondly, I would point out a basic principle that has served me well throughout my life: We have nothing to fear from the truth. I am reminded of Pres. Dieter F. Uchtdorf's remarks in the October 2013 General Conference:

> Sometimes there is a difference of opinion as to what the "facts" really mean. A question that creates doubt in some can, after careful investigation, build faith in others.[196]

And that is what I expect will happen here. Anyone whose testimony crumbles upon learning that the General Authorities are mere mortals has a testimony built on sand to start with, and needs to rebuild a spiritually based testimony, not one built on either emotion, intellect, or tradition.

---

[195] The irony of the situation here shall pass without remark.
[196] Uchtdorf (2013) p. 22.

"Old news."

It is hard to see the point of this objection, which has actually been made to me. Yes, many of these points were made twenty years ago and more, in scholarly articles and, to a much lesser extent, in a history of the Relief Society published by Deseret Book,[197] which quoted Joseph Smith's 1842 teachings without following their implications. But there is a new generation in the Church these days, who are largely unaware of the discussion as it stood in, say, the 1990s or earlier. (Much the same could be said of many older Saints.) We all deserve to have the opportunity to give these matters further consideration.

"So who are you, anyway, Mr. Author to say all this?"

No doubt some readers will point out that I am neither a General nor any manner of local Authority, and ask what business I have being an "Ark steadier." Fair enough.

I claim no authority. I do, however, claim the right to read, and to point out to others what I have read. I have not dictated action to the Church here. All I have done is to point out what the Standard Works say—and don't say—and what modern revelation says—and doesn't say—and what some good-as-lost teachings of Joseph Smith say, as these have been issued online over the last two years or so, as I write these words. I have a right to do this, even a responsibility to do so, if the scriptures are to be believed.[198]

If quoting scripture, modern revelation, and the words of the Prophet Joseph Smith amounts to being an "Ark steadier," then we as a Church have arrived at quite a sorry pass indeed. Oh, and one other thing:

That's *"Brother* Author," to you.

---

[197] Derr, Cannon, & Beecher (1992/2000).
[198] D&C 58:26-29.

"Why, you're just a <u>*<fill in the blank>*</u>."

I can easily imagine some readers taking issue with me personally because of what I have written here. For example, whether to my face or not, some readers might say that I am "just another—"

- "... liberal / intellectual." But do such readers even know what those words mean?

- "... person with a weak testimony." Ah, if only such readers knew just how wrong they are.

- "...pushy New Yorker." Guilty as charged, but irrelevant.

- "... trend-follower, seeking to obtain the praise of the world." Oh, really? Believe me, if I wanted to follow trends and obtain the praise of the world, absolutely the last thing I would ever have done would be to convert to Mormonism, let alone live it today.

This whole line of objection reminds me of a rather mean-spirited joke that circulates in the legal profession: "If you are arguing a case in court, and the law is against you, argue the facts of the case. If you can't argue from the facts of the case, argue from the law. If you can't argue the facts *or* the law—well, then, call the other lawyer names."

And so we see it so often in the Church today, in Sunday School classes, priesthood classes, and (or so I am told) Relief Society classes: During the class discussion, someone puts forth a point that is not in line with whatever the received wisdom is in the group. Instead of actually engaging the idea, one of more people resort to labelling, perhaps in private, perhaps in public.

Another newsflash: When people resort to labelling another person with some sort of pejorative term (or a term that they mean to be a put-down, whether or not it actually is), those people have just admitted that they are incapable of dealing with the issue at hand. Technically, this is called an *ad hominem* attack (an attack directed "to the person" rather than to an idea); it is one of the lowest forms of discourse, and it is an admission of ignorance. It is basically the same as saying, "I either don't know the facts, or I am not intellectually strong enough to actually deal with what you have to say." So, before anyone goes off and labels someone this way, it might be wise to think: "Is this something that I want to admit about myself?"

Not to mention, the Lord's position on this kind of reaction is very clear: "If ye are not one, ye are not mine."[199] Being "one" does not mean being in perfect agreement—perusing the records of discussions among the 19th Century Quorum of the Twelve should swiftly disabuse anyone of that notion—but it does mean treating each other with respect. Certainty that should not be too much to ask of people who style themselves as *Saints*.

---

[199] D&C 38:27.

7

Summary and Conclusion

In the Spring of 1842, Joseph Smith not only organized the Relief Society, but he also clearly stated that he wished to make of it a "kingdom of priests." He spoke of conveying "the keys to the kingdom" to the leadership of the Relief Society, and then said that he "turn[ed] the key to you," all of which I described in Chapter 1.

Unfortunately, as I related in Chapter 4, several factors combined to keep Joseph's doctrinal development about women and priesthood from being fully implemented. Joseph himself was assassinated. Emma Smith's strident teaching against the principle of plural marriage during Joseph's life, and her failure to support the Apostles' leadership after his death, alienated her from the new leadership of the Church. Emma subsequently defected from the Saints. Brigham Young, who may not even have been aware of Joseph's doctrinal development in this area, was certainly made wary of anything involving women in leadership capacities, because of Emma's leadership activities in Nauvoo, and subsequent defection. Finally, the *Nauvoo Relief Society Minute Book*, which recorded Joseph Smith's innovative teachings on women and priesthood, was unavailable to the public until June 2012.

When it comes to the Standard Works, there is no divinely ordained template that restricts the priesthood to men, or that bars women from the priesthood. The scriptural record is silent as to why women were not recorded as receiving the priesthood in the days of the patriarchs, or the early Christian Church. As I point out in Chapters 2 and 3, the cultures in these earlier eras would not have been receptive to or respectful of Gospel-believing women who held the priesthood.

In our day, the Church faces multiple crises regarding the present policy regarding women and the priesthood, crises that have and will continue to have impact on the growth of the Church (see Chapter 5). In a day and age when women in Western industrialized societies are vastly more educated than they were in the 1840s, and have much more in the way of civil rights, women expect to be able to exert their leadership skills and abilities in all areas of life. Not being able to do this in the Church is a cause of pain to many LDS women. This pain, and a situation in which policies about the priesthood have been implemented without any real evidence of divine mandate, are major factors in the defection of many Saints, men and women, from the Church. In addition, the LDS priesthood policy—without any scriptural or revelatory justification—simply looks sexist on the face of it, which likely is alienating to many potential coverts.

However, the very existence of these crises may itself provoke the Brethren to seek to the Lord in prayer, resulting in a change in policy (much as what occurred with the reversal of the racial priesthood restriction). In the meantime, I suggest that the Saints do not try to force the Lord's or the Prophet's hand; that they pray for the Lord to clarify this matter; that they frame the matter of women and the priesthood, not as 'they can't have it,' but as 'they *will* have it,' a position that is perfectly consistent with latter-day Gospel teaching. I also suggest that we can do things now to integrate women more fully into the local councils of the Church, and to familiarize the Church with the teachings of Joseph Smith to the Nauvoo Relief Society. In addition, I suggest that we make it a more prominent part of LDS culture that, when people make doctrinal claims, we ask: "Where does it say that?", in the hopes that (to reverse the old Hermetic adage) "As below, so above."

There are several forms that a priesthood with women might take. The important thing to remember is that, as scripture teaches, all offices are merely appendages to the Priesthood itself. It will be exciting to see what the Lord will do in relation to women and the priesthood—if only we have the ears to hear.

We have been on something of a journey. I have come out of it with a more brightly burning testimony of the Gospel, and how could I not? I've been working with the scriptures, the words of Joseph Smith, and the writings of others of the prophets, in order to write this book. I hope that you, as a reader, will have felt some of that spirit as well.

References

Notes. As is common practice, the word "The" is not considered in placing these entries in alphabetical order by author or title. Hence, "The Pew Forum ..." is alphabetized under the letter *P*.

Citations with two dates separated by a slash (such as "Derr, Cannon, & Beecher 1992/2000") were originally published on the earlier date but reprinted in a new edition on the later date. They are found in the References section under the *later* date.

The LDS Standard Works—the Holy Bible, the Book of Mormon, the Doctrine and Covenants, and the Pearl of Great Price—are each available for consultation online at https://www.lds.org/scriptures ; they do not appear separately among the references listed below.

2013 Church almanac. (2012). Salt Lake City, UT: Deseret News.

Arrington, L. J. (1986). *Brigham Young: American Moses.* Urbana, IL: University of Illinois Press. (Original work published 1985)

Beard, M., North, J., & Price, S. (1998). *Religions of Rome. Volume 1: A history.* Cambridge, England, UK: Cambridge University Press.

Bloom, H. (1992). *The American religion: The emergence of the post-Christian nation.* New York, NY: Simon & Schuster.

Brown, F., Driver, S. R., & Briggs, C. A. (1951). *A Hebrew and English lexicon of the Old Testament.* Oxford, England, UK: Clarendon Press / Oxford University Press. (Original work published 1906)

Bruni, F. (2014, April 13). Women's unequal lot. *The New York Times,* Sunday Review p. 3.

Bush, L. E., Jr. (1969, Winter). A commentary on Stephen G. Taggart's *Mormonism's Negro policy: Social and historical origins. Dialogue: A Journal of Mormon Thought,* 4(4), 86-103. Online at https://www.dialoguejournal.com/wp-content/uploads/sbi/issues/V04N04.pdf [Note: This paper—less its Appendix—is also collected in Bush & Mauss, 1984.]

Bush, L. E., Jr. (1973). Mormonism's Negro doctrine: An historical overview. *Dialogue: A Journal of Mormon Thought, 8*(1) 11-68. Online at https://www.dialoguejournal.com/wp-content/uploads/sbi/articles/Dialogue_V08N01_13.pdf pdf [Note: This paper also collected in Bush & Mauss, 1984.]

Bush, L. E., Jr., & Mauss, A. L. (Eds.). (1984). *Neither white nor black: Mormon scholars confront the race issue in a universal church.* Salt Lake City, UT: Signature Books. Full text online at http://signaturebookslibrary.org/?p=438

Bushman, R. L. (2005). *Joseph Smith: Rough stone rolling.* New York, NY: Knopf.

Charles, M. M.. (1985, Fall). Scriptural precedents for priesthood. *Dialogue: A Journal of Mormon Thought, 18*(3), 15-21. Online at http://www.dialoguejournal.com/wp-content/uploads/sbi/articles/Dialogue_V18N03_17.pdf

Collins, G. (2007). *America's women: 400 years of dolls, drudges, helpmates, and heroines.* New York: HarperCollins. (Original work published 2003)

"Compass interview with President Gordon B. Hinckley" [online transcript of television interview]. (1997, November 9). Online at http://www.abc.net.au/compass/intervs/hinckley.htm

Daughters in my kingdom: The history and work of Relief Society. (2011). Salt Lake City, UT: The Church of Jesus Christ of Latter-day Saints. Online at https://www.lds.org/relief-society/daughters-in-my-kingdom

Dening, S. (1996). *The mythology of sex.* New York, NY: Macmillan.

Derr, J. M., Cannon, J. R., & Beecher, M. U. (2000). *Women of covenant: The story of Relief Society.* Salt Lake City, UT: Deseret Book. (Original work published 1992)

Derr, J., & Madsen, C. C. (2005). "Something better" for the sisters: Joseph Smith and the Female Relief Society of Nauvoo. In *Joseph*

Smith and the doctrinal Restoration: The 34*th* Annual Sidney B. Sperry Symposium* (pp. 123-143). Provo, UT: Brigham Young University, Religious Studies Center. Papers in this volume are online at http://rsc.byu.edu/archived/joseph-smith-and-doctrinal-restoration/

Dew, S. (2013). *Women and the priesthood: What one Mormon woman believes*. Salt Lake City, UT: Deseret Book Company.

Doctrine and Covenants Student Manual: Religion 324 and 325 (2nd ed.). (2001). Salt Lake City, UT: The Church of Jesus Christ of Latter-day Saints. Online at http://institute.lds.org/manuals/doctrine-and-covenants

Ehat, A. F., & Cook, L. W. (Eds.). (1991). *The words of Joseph Smith: The contemporary accounts of the Nauvoo discourses of the Prophet Joseph*. n.p.: Grandin Book Company. (Original work published 1980, Provo, UT: Religious Studies Center, Brigham Young University). The Grandin edition is online at https://archive.org/details/TheWordsOfJosephSmith . Text of the Religious Studies Center edition, apparently with some edits from the original print edition, online at https://rsc.byu.edu/out-print/words-joseph-smith-contemporary-accounts-nauvoo-discourses-prophet-joseph

The First Presidency and Council of the Twelve Apostles of The Church of Jesus Christ of Latter-day Saints. (1995). *The family: A proclamation to the world*. Online at https://www.lds.org/topics/family-proclamation and at https://www.lds.org/bc/content/shared/content/english/pdf/36035_000_24_family.pdf

Fowler, F. J., Jr. (2002). *Survey research methods* (3rd ed.). Thousand Oaks, CA: Sage Publications.

Frier, B. W., & McGinn, T. A. J. (2004). *A casebook on Roman family law*. New York, NY: Oxford University Press.

Gospel principles. (2009). Salt Lake City, UT: The Church of Jesus Christ of Latter-day Saints. Online at https://www.lds.org/manual/gospel-principles

Gula, R. J. (2002). *Nonsense: A handbook of logical fallacies*. Mount Jackson, VA: Axios Press.

Hedges, A. H., Smith, A. D., & Anderson, R. L. (Eds.). (2011). *The Joseph Smith Papers: Journals Vol. 2. December 1841-April 1843*. Salt Lake City, UT: The Church Historian's Press, The Church History Department, The Church of Jesus Christ of Latter-day Saints. The entry for 17 March 1842 is online at http://josephsmithpapers.org/paperSummary/journal-december-1841-december-1842?p=22 . The entry for 28 April 1840 is online at http://josephsmithpapers.org/paperSummary/journal-december-1841-december-1842?locale=eng&p=25

Henderson, P., & Cooke, K. (2012, January 31). Special Report: Mormons besieged by the modern age [online news story]. *Reuters*. Online at http://www.reuters.com/article/2012/01/31/us-mormonchurch-idUSTRE80T1CM20120131

Herbert-Brown, G. (1994). *Ovid and the Fasti: An historical study*. New York, NY: Oxford University Press.

"High priest: Summary" [web page]. (2014). *The Joseph Smith Papers*. Accessed April 25, 2014. Online at http://josephsmithpapers.org/topic/high-priest

History, 1838-1856, Volume C-1 Addenda [part of the Manuscript History of the Church]. (written 1854). Online at http://josephsmithpapers.org/paperSummary/history-1838-1856-volume-c-1-addenda

History of the Church [full-title: *History of The Church of Jesus Christ of Latter-day Saints*]. (1902-1932). (7 vols.; B. H. Roberts, Ed.). Salt Lake City, UT: Deseret News. Volume 4 online at http://books.google.com/books?id=UO0gMzekGP4C&hl=en

Hymowitz, C., & Weissman, M. (1978). *A history of women in America*. New York, NY: Bantam Books.

Jessee, D. C. (1971). The writing of Joseph Smith's history. *BYU Studies, 11*(4), 439-473. Online at https://byustudies.byu.edu/showtitle.aspx?title=4976

Jessee, D. C. (1976). The reliability of Joseph Smith's history. *Journal of Mormon History, 3*, 23-46. Online at http://digitalcommons.usu.edu/mormonhistory/vol3/iss1/1/

JPS Hebrew-English Tanakh. (1999). Philadelphia, PA: Jewish Publication Society.

Kimball, E. L. (2005). *Lengthen your stride: The presidency of Spencer W. Kimball.* Salt Lake City, UT: Deseret Book.

Kimball, E. L. (2008). Spencer W. Kimball and the revelation on priesthood. *BYU Studies, 47*(2), 5-78. Online at https://ojs.lib.byu.edu/spc/index.php/BYUStudies/article/viewFile/7325/6974

Lipka, M. (2013, October 8). Big majority of Mormons (including women) oppose women in priesthood [online press release]. *FactTank: News in the Numbers* [website]. Online at the website of the Pew Research Center, http://www.pewresearch.org/fact-tank/2013/10/08/big-majority-of-mormons-oppose-women-in-priesthood-including-women/

"Louis CK Monologue" [website with video clip]. (2014, March 29). As of April 15, 2014, this was online at http://www.nbc.com/saturday-night-live/video/louis-ck-monologue/2768583

Mauss, A. L. (1967, Winter). Mormonism and the Negro: Faith, folklore and civil rights. *Dialogue: A Journal of Mormon Thought, 2*(4), 19-39. Online at https://www.dialoguejournal.com/archive/issue-details/?in=8 . [Note: This paper is also collected in Bush & Mauss, 1984.]

Mauss, A. L. (1981). The fading of the Pharaohs' curse: The decline and fall of the priesthood ban against Blacks in the Mormon Church. *Dialogue: A Journal of Mormon Thought, 14*(3), 10-45. Online at https://www.dialoguejournal.com/wp-content/uploads/sbi/articles/Dialogue_V14N03_12.pdf . [Note: This paper is also collected in Bush & Mauss, 1984.]

McBaine, N. (2012, Fall). To do the business of the Church: A cooperative paradigm for examining gendered participation within Church organizational structure. *Dialogue: A Journal of Mormon Thought, 45*(3), 70-97. Online at https://www.dialoguejournal.com/archive/dialogue-premium-content/fall-2012/ [behind a paywall]. Text of original conference presentation is online at http://www.fairmormon.org/perspectives/fair-conferences/2012-fair-conference/2012-to-do-the-business-of-the-church-a-cooperative-paradigm

Mormon Research Foundation. (2012). *Understanding Mormon disbelief: Why do some Mormons lose their testimony, and what happens to them when they do?* [online document]. Online at http://www.whymormonsquestion.org/wp-content/uploads/2012/05/Survey-Results_Understanding-Mormon-Disbelief-Mar20121.pdf

Nauvoo Relief Society Minute Book. (1842-1844). Online at http://josephsmithpapers.org/paperSummary/nauvoo-relief-society-minute-book?locale=eng&p=1 . [Note: best viewed using the Chrome or Firefox browsers.]

Newell, L. K. (1985, Autumn). The historical relationship between Mormon women and priesthood. *Dialogue: A Journal of Mormon Thought, 18*(3), 21-32. Online at http://www.dialoguejournal.com/wp-content/uploads/sbi/articles/Dialogue_V18N03_23.pdf

Oaks, D. H. (1992, May). The Relief Society and the Church. *Ensign* [electronic edition]. Online at https://www.lds.org/ensign/print/1992/05/the-relief-society-and-the-church

Olson, C. F. (2011a). Ten Commandments. In R. L. Millet, C. F. Olson, A. C. Skinner, & B. L. Top, *LDS beliefs: A doctrinal reference* (pp. 617-618). Salt Lake City, UT: Deseret Book.

Olson, C. F. (2011b). Woman. In R. L. Millet, C. F. Olson, A. C. Skinner, & B. L. Top, *LDS beliefs: A doctrinal reference* (pp. 661-665). Salt Lake City, UT: Deseret Book.

Paul, R., & Elder, L. (n.d.). *The miniature guide to critical thinking: Concepts & tools* [pamphlet]. Dillon Beach, CA: The Foundation for Critical Thinking.

The Pew Forum on Religion & Public Life. (2012). *2011 National Survey of Mormons: Final Questionnaire.* Online at http://www.pewforum.org/files/2012/01/Mormons-in-America-Questionnaire-.pdf

Pew Research Center. (2012, January 12). *Mormons in America: Certain in their beliefs, uncertain of their place in society.* Washington, DC: Pew Research Center, Pew Forum on Religion

& Public Life. Online at http://www.pewforum.org/files/2012/01/Mormons-in-America.pdf

Prince, G. A., & Wright, W. R. (2005). *David O. McKay and the rise of modern Mormonism*. Salt Lake City, UT: University of Utah Press.

Quinn, D. M. (1992). Mormon women have had the priesthood since 1843. In Maxine Hanks (ed.), *Women and authority: Re-emerging Mormon feminism* (pp. 365-409). Salt Lake City, UT: Signature Books. This entire book is available online at http://signaturebookslibrary.org/?p=840; this portion (Chapter 17) is available at http://signaturebookslibrary.org/?p=1171

"Race and the Priesthood" (web page). (2013, December 6). Online at https://www.lds.org/topics/race-and-the-priesthood

"R.S. Reports." (1880, September 1). *The Woman's Exponent, 9*(7), pp. 53 [mistakenly labelled "55"]-54. Online at http://contentdm.lib.byu.edu/cdm/compoundobject/collection/WomansExp/id/7688/rec/199

"R.S. Reports: Pioneer Stake." (1905, July and August). *Woman's Exponent, 34*(2-3), p. 14. Online at http://contentdm.lib.byu.edu/cdm/compoundobject/collection/WomansExp/id/32331/rec/696

Saller, R. P. (1993). Roman empire. In B. M. Metzger & M. D. Coogan (Eds.), *The Oxford guide to the Bible* (pp. 657-659). New York, NY: Oxford University Press.

"Salt Lake Stake Relief Society Conference." (1880, July 1). *The Woman's Exponent, 9*(3), pp. 21-22. Online at http://contentdm.lib.byu.edu/cdm/compoundobject/collection/WomansExp/id/7370/rec/195

Scheid, J. (2003). *An introduction to Roman religion* (Janet Lloyd, Trans.) Bloomington, IN: Indiana University Press.

Schultz, C. E. (2006). *Women's religious activity in the Roman Republic*. Chapel Hill, NC: University of North Carolina Press.

Septuaginta (A. Rahlfs, ed., 1 volume edition). (1979). Stuttgart, Germany: Deutsche Bibelgesellschaft.

Smith, Alison Moore. (2014, March 29). Do Mormon women oppose priesthood ordination? Clarity about the Pew survey [blog post].

Mormon Momma: Crossing the plains in the modern world [website]. Online at http://www.mormonmomma.com/index.php/2014/do-mormon-women-oppose-priesthood-ordination-pew-survey/

Smith, Joseph Fielding (Ed.). (1938). *Teachings of the Prophet Joseph Smith*. Salt Lake City, UT: Deseret Book Company. Text of the book, giving page numbers of the print edition, online at http://www.boap.org/LDS/Joseph-Smith/Teachings/

Smith, Joseph Fielding. (1941, September). The spirit of reverence and worship. *The Improvement Era, 44*(9), pp. 525, 572-573, 575. Online at https://archive.org/details/improvementera4409unse

Smith, Joseph Fielding. (1954-1956). *Doctrines of salvation: Sermons and writings of Joseph Fielding Smith* (3 vols.). Salt Lake City, UT: Bookcraft.

Smith, Joseph Fielding. (1959, January). Relief Society—An aid to the Priesthood. *The Relief Society Magazine, 46*(1), pp. 4-6. Online at https://archive.org/details/reliefsocietymag46reli

Smith, Julie M. (2014, March 19). A kingdom of priests [blog post]. *Times and Seasons* [website]. Online at http://timesandseasons.org/index.php/2014/03/a-kingdom-of-priests/

Sperling, H., & Simon, M. (Trans.). (1984). *The Zohar: Vol. 2* (2nd ed.). London, England, UK: The Soncino Press.

"Statistical Report, 2013." (2014, May). *Ensign*. Online at https://www.lds.org/ensign/2014/05/saturday-afternoon-session/statistical-report-2013

Taylor, J. (1858). The rights of Mormonism: August 30, 1857. *Journal of Discourses*, Vol. 5. Liverpool & London, England, UK: Latter-day Saints' Book Depot. Consulted on *New Mormon Studies CD-ROM: A Comprehensive Resource Library, 2009 Edition*. Salt Lake City, UT: Signature Books.

Taylor, J. (1987). *The gospel kingdom: Selections from the writings and discourses of John Taylor, third president of The Church of Jesus Christ of Latter-day Saints* (G. H. Durham, ed.; collector's ed.). Salt Lake City, Bookcraft. (Original work published 1941)

Teachings of Presidents of the Church: Joseph Smith. (2007). Salt Lake City, UT: The Church of Jesus Christ of Latter-day Saints. Online at https://www.lds.org/manual/teachings-joseph-smith

True to the faith: A gospel reference. (2004). Salt Lake City, UT: The Church of Jesus Christ of Latter-day Saints. Online at https://www.lds.org/bc/content/shared/content/english/pdf/language-materials/36863_eng.pdf

Uchtdorf, D. F. (2013, November). Come, join with us. *Ensign*, 43(11), pp. 21-24. Online at https://www.lds.org/ensign/2013/11

U.S. and World Population Clock [website]. (2014, April 21). Online, updated in real time, at http://www.census.gov/popclock/

"Why do you no longer believe that the LDS church is the true church?" [online survey]. (n.d.). Accessed April 24, 2014 at http://psychmeasures.org/index.php?sid=58166&newtest=Y&lang=en

"Women in the Church" [web page]. Accessed April 25, 2014. Online at https://www.lds.org/topics/women-in-the-church

Illustration Credits

Figure 1-1. Detail of *Relief Society Magazine*, March 1936, front cover, by Joseph A. F. Everett. Public domain. Volume 23 (1936) online at https://archive.org/details/reliefsocietymag36reli

Figure 1-2. Work of the author.

Figure 2-1. This is modified from the file "Roman Empire map-2.gif" created by Wikipedia user "Swarm." It appears here under the Creative Commons Attribution-Share Alike 3.0 Unported (http://creativecommons.org/licenses/by-sa/3.0/deed.en) license. The original file is located at http://en.wikipedia.org/wiki/File:Roman_Empire_map-2.gif .

Index

19th century, xii, 34, 39
20th century, 83, 114
21st century, 39, 51, 93
Abraham, 8, 44, 45, 46, 50
Alma, 4
Arrington, Leonard J., 112
Articles of Faith, 87
Asherah, 45
attrition, LDS, 89, 94, 97, 120
Babylonian empire, 44
Bible, 4, 7, 19, 41, 42, 45, 48, 61, 62, 123
Bloom, Harold, 114
Book of Abraham, 77
Book of Mormon, xii, 4, 41, 50, 98, 123
Brazil, 89
Brigham Young University, 101
Bryn Mawr College, 98
Church of Jesus Christ of Latter-day Saints, The, xii, 3, 59, 76
Commandments, Ten, 18, 47, 49
Comprehensive History of the Church (B. H. Roberts), 34
Council of Fifty, 79
crises arising from barring women from the priesthood, 89, 99
    basis, 89

crisis in sharing the Gospel, 98
crisis of pain, 93
crisis of testimony and defection, 95
Daughters in My Kingdom (book), 84, 85
defection, LDS. *See* attrition, LDS
Dew, Sheri, 89
Dimmuzi. *See* Dumuzi
Doctrine and Covenants, 6, 41, 114, 123
Dumuzi, 44
Elias, 7, 8
Elijah, 7, 8
    called Elias, 7
endowment, LDS temple, 9, 10, 20, 76, 77, 79
Enoch, vi, 4, 14, 18, 21, 30, 35, 69, 85
Enoch, Book of, 21
Entu, 44
Europe, 99
exaltation, 5, 6
Fordham University, xiii, 137
God
    mind of, Joseph Smith on, 109
Gospel of Jesus Christ, xi, 3, 59
Haverford College, xiii, 98, 102, 137

133

hieros gamos ceremony, 44
Hinckley, Gordon B., 64, 66
History of the Church (7 vols., ed. by B. H. Roberts), 26, 29, 31, 32, 34, 35, 36, 37, 38, 39
Hudson, Valerie, 105
Ifediba, Titus, 88
Inanna, 44
Ishtar, 44
ishtaritu, 44
Japan Okayama Mission (LDS), xiii, 137
Jesus Christ, xii, 7, 49, 50, 52
    transfiguration of, 7
Joseph Smith Papers Project, 32, 34, 84, 107
key
    Joseph Smith turns the key to the Nauvoo Relief Society Presidency, vi, 17, 22, 25, 28, 30, 37, 77, 84
keys
    Joseph Smith speaks of delivering, to Relief Society and Church, 16, 22, 30, 36
    priesthood, 6
keys of the kingdom
    definition, 6
    delivered to Peter, James, and John, 6, 7
    Emma's, nullified, 28, 75, 82, 86
    Joseph Smith delivered to the Quorum of the Twelve, 8, 9, 79, 82
    Joseph Smith receives, in the Kirtland Temple, 7
    Joseph Smith's statement that he was about to give, to Nauvoo Relief Society Presidency, vi, 21, 22, 23, 25, 29, 30, 75, 77, 84, 85
Kimball, Spencer W., 89, 114
King Follett discourse, 79, 113
kingdom of priestesses, 20, 77
kingdom of priests
    Geo. A. Smith recasts Joseph's statement about, 35
    Joseph Smith's aim to make Nauvoo Relief Society a, vi, 14, 18, 20, 29, 30, 35, 69, 75, 77, 85, 119
    scriptural phrase, 18, 19, 20
Kirtland apostasy, 97
Kirtland Temple (LDS), 7, 76
Koltko-Rivera, Mark, 137
    conversion, xii
    family response to conversion, xii
    learns of reversal of racial priesthood restriction, 88
    research regarding racial priesthood restriction coverage in media, 102
    testimony, xii, 10, 121
Lee, Harold B., 57, 63, 115
Luman, Richard, 102
Manhattan (New York City), 137
Manuscript History of the Church, viii, 26, 32, 33, 34, 35, 36, 37, 38, 39

Index

McBaine, Neylan, 93, 106

Mormon Research Foundation survey, 95, 97

Mosaic Law, 20, 47, 49, 50, 52

Moses, 7, 8, 18, 20, 44, 46, 47, 48, 49, 50, 60

Nauvoo Relief Society Minute Book, iv, vi, 13, 14, 16, 17, 20, 22, 23, 26, 28, 29, 31, 32, 35, 36, 37, 38, 39, 68, 69, 83, 84, 85, 107, 109, 113, 114, 119, 128

Nauvoo Temple (LDS), 76, 77

New York City, xiv, 27, 88, 91, 98, 137

New York University, xiii, 137

Newell, Linda King, 22

Nigeria, 89, 101

Paul, vi, 14, 18, 20, 21, 30, 35, 49, 50, 53, 61, 62, 63, 69, 85

Pearl of Great Price, 21, 42, 87, 113, 123

Pew Forum on Religion and Public Life, survey by, 67, 68, 69, 70

Priesthood
Aaronic, 46, 47, 50, 52
definition, 3
elder, office of, 76
high priest, office of, 76
Melchizedek, 5, 42, 43, 44, 46, 48, 52, 108
offices, merely appendages to the, 108
racial restriction, former, 87, 88, 101, 102, 103, 107, 111, 113, 120

revelation needed to extend, to women, 100
royal, a (scriptural phrase), 19
true name, 109
women, with, 107

principles
change something, build a new model, to, 103
upper world moves in response to the lower world, the, 103
you don't ask, you don't get, 27

qideshah, 45, 46

Quorum of the Twelve Apostles (LDS), 8, 22, 39, 49, 57, 62, 65, 80, 118

Relief Society, Nauvoo
implications of what Joseph Smith taught to, 27
Joseph Smith's teachings to. *See* key; keys; keys of the kingdom, Joseph Smith's statement …; kingdom of priests, Joseph Smith's aim …

retcon. *See* retroactive continuity (retcon)

retroactive continuity (retcon), 25, 26
definition, 13, 25
examples, 13, 25, 26, 36, 37, 38

Rhinebeck, NY, xii

Roberts, B. H., 32, 34

Roman Empire, viii, 53, 54, 56

Rome, 53, 55, 56

Salt Lake City, Utah, 65, 106

salvation, 3, 4, 5, 6, 9, 62

Septuagint, 19

Smith, Alison Moore, 70

Smith, Bathsheba W., 20, 23, 29, 83

Smith, Emma Hale, 22, 75, 78, 80, 81, 82, 83, 86, 119
  keys nullified, 28, 75, 82, 86

Smith, George A., 25, 26, 28, 31, 39

Smith, Joseph, iv, vi, vii, viii, ix, x, xii, xiv, 3, 4, 5, 7, 8, 9, 13, 14, 17, 18, 20, 21, 22, 23, 24, 25, 26, 27, 28, 29, 30, 31, 32, 34, 35, 36, 37, 38, 39, 42, 48, 56, 57, 60, 61, 62, 63, 69, 75, 76, 77, 78, 79, 80, 81, 82, 83, 84, 85, 86, 87, 88, 97, 105, 107, 108, 109, 113, 114, 115, 116, 119, 120, 121, 130
  helical pattern of doctrinal development, 27, 76, 77
  teachings to Nauvoo Relief Society. *See:* key; keys; keys of the kingdom, Joseph Smith's statement ...; kingdom of priests, Joseph Smith's aim ...

teachings, implications of, 27

Smith, Joseph Fielding, 49, 57, 58, 62, 63, 115, 130

Smith, Julie M., 18

Snow Smith, Eliza Roxcy, 18, 25, 29, 35, 39, 83

Standard Works (LDS), ix, 10, 41, 42, 52, 60, 68, 73, 79, 88, 115, 116, 119, 123, *See also*: Bible, Book of Mormon, Doctrine and Covenants, Pearl of Great Price

Sumer, 44, 45

Tammuz, 44

Taylor, John, 65, 66, 81, 106, 108

Teachings of the Prophet Joseph Smith (book), 31, 34, 36, 37, 39

Uchtdorf, Dieter F., 58, 59, 115

United States of America, 39, 90, 95, 99, 114

Women of Covenant (book), 29

Young, Brigham, 8, 75, 80, 82, 83, 84, 86, 87, 90, 111, 119

Zohar (multivolume book), 103

About the Author

Mark Koltko-Rivera converted to The Church of Jesus Christ of Latter-day Saints while attending Haverford College in Pennsylvania. He served for two years as an LDS missionary in the Japan Okayama Mission. He has served in the Church as a home teacher, a Gospel Doctrine Sunday School teacher, a bishop's counselor in two wards, and a member of a stake high council. He has published about the Latter-day Saints in *Sunstone*, *Dialogue*, and *Psychotherapy*.

Mark Koltko-Rivera holds a doctoral degree from the Department of Applied Psychology at New York University (NYU). He is an elected Fellow of the American Psychological Association. For his scholarship, he has received several awards: the Margaret Gorman Early Career Award in the psychology of religion (from the Society for the Psychology of Religion and Spirituality), the Carmi Harari Early Career Award for Inquiry (Society for Humanistic Psychology), and, on two occasions, the George A. Miller Award for an outstanding recent article on general psychology (Society for General Psychology). He has taught at NYU, the University of Central Florida and elsewhere.

He was born and raised on the Lower East Side of Manhattan in New York City, where he long lived in the East Village. He graduated from Regis High School (NYC), and holds an undergraduate degree from Haverford College and a master's degree from Fordham University.

Dr. Koltko-Rivera has four grown children and four grandchildren (and counting). He lives in New York City, where he is active in the Church. He is the author of *The Rise of the Mormons: Latter-day Saint Growth in the 21st Century* (2012), the second edition of which is expected to be issued during the summer of 2014.

His website and e-mail address are listed at the conclusion of the Preface of this book.

www.ingramcontent.com/pod-product-compliance
Lightning Source LLC
Chambersburg PA
CBHW060833050426
42453CB00008B/679